THE
PASSION
TRANSLATION

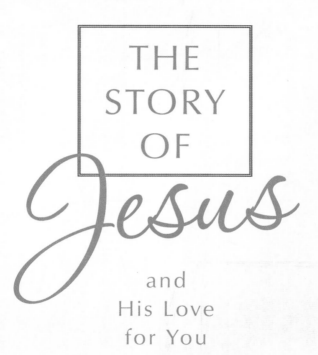

THE
STORY
OF

Jesus

and
His Love
for You

BroadStreet
PUBLISHING

THE STORY OF *Jesus* and His Love for You

Published by BroadStreet Publishing® Group, LLC
Racine, Wisconsin, USA
BroadStreetPublishing.com

© 2018 BroadStreet Publishing Group

ISBN-13: 978-1-4245-5625-0 (faux leather)
ISBN-13: 978-1-4245-5219-1 (e-book)

Cover by Garborg Design Works, Inc.
Interior typesetting by Katherine Lloyd

Printed in China
18 19 20 21 22   5 4 3 2 1

Contents

Introduction

How God longs for us to know him! We discover him as we read and study his living Word. But the "Word" is not just dead letters; it's the Living Expression of God, Jesus Christ. The Word came with skin on as the Perfect Man— the One who is the divine self-expression and fullness of God's glory; he was God in the flesh!

The Story of Jesus tells the story of this God-in-the-Flesh Man through the eyes of one of his closest friends and followers, John. Some people know this book as the Gospel of John, because it tells the "good news" or gospel about Jesus. John's book unveils Jesus as the Son of God sent to give life to the world.

The books of Matthew, Mark, and Luke in the Bible give us the *history* of Jesus, but John writes to unveil the *mystery* of Jesus. Jesus is seen as the Lamb of God, the Good Shepherd, the Kind Forgiver, the Tender Healer, the Compassionate Intercessor, and the Great I Am. Who can resist this man when he tugs on your heart to come to him?

To read John's gospel is to encounter Jesus. Make this your goal as you read his story.

HE WILL TAKE AWAY
THE SINS OF THE WORLD!

When Jesus was first introduced to his community, a local prophet named John the Immerser (a different John than the author of the book of John) said some startling words about Jesus: "Look! There he is—God's Lamb! He will take away the sins of the world! I told you that a Mighty One would come who is far greater than I am, because he existed long before I was born!" (1:29-30)

What a strange nickname: the Lamb of God! Yet it makes perfect sense when you understand our human story better.

IT IS FINISHED!

All of us are born with a problem: we all have sinned, which has separated us from a relationship with God. So something needed to be done with these acts and our guilt.

That's where Jesus comes in! Jesus took away our sins in the most unlikely way imaginable. One of the most well-known verses in the Bible is found in *The Story of Jesus*. Perhaps you've seen it on poster boards wielded by fans at national sporting events. The verse is John 3:16, and it goes like this:

> For this is how much God loved the world—he gave his one and only, unique Son as a gift. So now everyone who believes in him will never perish but experience everlasting life.

God gave Jesus as a gift to take away our sins—forever. But what is the gift of Jesus? Some say it's his example of love and his teachings. Yes, that's true, but it's deeper than that. John wrote, "God did not send his Son into the world to judge and condemn the world, but to be its Savior and rescue it!" (3:17)

That's the gift of Jesus!

Amazingly Jesus provided this gift himself by dying for the sins of the world. Toward the end of Jesus' story, he was condemned for crimes he didn't commit. As his punishment he was crucified, nailed through both hands and feet on a cross—like a lamb led to the slaughterhouse.

Because Jesus paid the price for our sins in our place, "now there is no longer any condemnation for those who believe in him" (3:18). He cried out just before he passed, "It is finished, my bride!" Everything that was necessary to take away your sins, release you from shame and guilt, and rescue you from death has been accomplished by Jesus!

SO THAT YOU WILL FULLY BELIEVE

John said he wrote his story about Jesus "so that you will fully believe that Jesus is the Anointed One, the Son of God, and that through your faith in him you will experience eternal life by the power of his name!" (20:31)

Do you believe that Jesus did everything necessary to make you right with God? That he defeated the brokenness and chaos of the world, and death itself? That he has a plan for your life and is the door to walking in all he has created you to be and do?

If not, we invite you to read the book of John and discover this Jesus for yourself. Invite God to speak to you as you read:

> Jesus, reveal yourself to me as I read the book of John.
> I want to experience you and the truth that brings true freedom. Come into my life and show me your way and the path you have for me.

You can trust every word you read from the book of John, for he speaks the truth. His story about Jesus will take you into a higher place where Jesus now sits at the right hand of God.

As John's gospel unveils Jesus before your eyes, enter into the great magnificence of his presence and sit with him. Your life will never be the same after absorbing the glory presented to you in *The Story of Jesus*!

The Book of John

The Living Expression

1 In the very beginning the Living Expression was already there.

And the Living Expression was with God, yet fully God.

2 They were together—face-to-face, in the very beginning.

3 And through his creative inspiration
this Living Expression made all things,
for nothing has existence apart from him!

4 Life came into being because of him,
for his life is light for all humanity.

5 And this Living Expression is the Light that bursts through gloom—
the Light that darkness could not diminish!

6 Then suddenly a man appeared who was sent from God,
a messenger named John.

7 For he came to be a witness, to point the way to the Light of Life,
and to help everyone believe.

8 John was not that Light but he came to show who is.
For he was merely a messenger to speak the truth about the Light.

9 For the Light of Truth was about to come into the world
and shine upon everyone.

10He entered into the very world he created,
   yet the world was unaware.
11He came to the very people he created—
   to those who should have recognized him,
   but they did not receive him.
12But those who embraced him and took hold of his name
   were given authority to become
   the children of God!
13He was not born by the joining of human parents
   or from natural means, or by a man's desire,
   but he was born of God.
14And so the Living Expression
   became a man and lived among us!
   And we gazed upon the splendor of his glory,
   the glory of the One and Only
   who came from the Father overflowing
   with tender mercy and truth!
15John taught the truth about him
   when he announced to the people,
   "He's the One! Set your hearts on him!
   I told you he would come after me,
   even though he ranks far above me,
   for he existed before I was even born."
16And now out of his fullness we are fulfilled!
   And from him we receive grace heaped upon more
      grace!
17Moses gave us the Law, but Jesus, the Anointed One,
   unveils truth wrapped in tender mercy.
18No one has ever gazed upon the fullness of God's
      splendor

except the uniquely beloved Son,
who is cherished by the Father
and held close to his heart.
Now he has unfolded to us
the full explanation of who God truly is!

The Ministry of John the Baptizer

¹⁹There were some of the Jewish leaders who sent an entourage of priests and temple servants from Jerusalem to interrogate John. They asked him, "Who are you?"

²⁰John answered them directly, saying, "I am not the Messiah!"

²¹"Then who are you?" they asked. "Are you Elijah?"

"No," John replied.

So they pressed him further, "Are you the prophet Moses said was coming, the one we're expecting?" "No," he replied.

²²"Then who are you?" they demanded. "We need an answer for those who sent us. Tell us something about yourself—anything!"

²³So, John answered them, "I am fulfilling Isaiah's prophecy: 'I am an urgent, thundering voice shouting in the desert—clear the way and prepare your hearts for the coming of the Lord Yahweh!'"

²⁴Then some members of the religious sect known as the Pharisees questioned John, ²⁵"Why do you baptize the people since you admit you're not the Christ, Elijah, or the Prophet?"

²⁶⁻²⁷John answered them, "I baptize in this river, but the One who will take my place is to be more honored than I,

but even when he stands among you, you will not recognize or embrace him! I am not worthy enough to stoop down in front of him and untie his sandals!" 28This all took place at Bethany, where John was baptizing at the place of the crossing of the Jordan River.

The Lamb of God

29The very next day John saw Jesus coming to him to be baptized, and John cried out, "Look! There he is—God's Lamb! He will take away the sins of the world! 30I told you that a Mighty One would come who is far greater than I am, because he existed long before I was born! 31My baptism was for the preparation of his appearing to Israel, even though I've yet to experience him."

32Then, as John baptized Jesus he spoke these words: "I see the Spirit of God appear like a dove descending from the heavenly realm and landing upon him—and it rested upon him from that moment forward! 33And even though I've yet to experience him, when I was commissioned to baptize with water God spoke these words to me, 'One day you will see the Spirit descend and remain upon a man. He will be the One I have sent to baptize with the Holy Spirit.' 34And now I have seen with discernment. I can tell you for sure that this man is the Son of God."

Jesus' First Followers

35-36The very next day John was there again with two of his disciples as Jesus was walking right past them. John, gazing upon him, pointed to Jesus and said, "Look! There's God's

Lamb!" ³⁷And as soon as John's two disciples heard this, they immediately left John and began to follow a short distance behind Jesus.

³⁸Then Jesus turned around and saw they were following him and asked, "What do you want?" They responded, "Rabbi (which means, Master Teacher), where are you staying?" ³⁹Jesus answered, "Come and discover for yourselves." So they went with him and saw where he was staying, and since it was late in the afternoon, they spent the rest of the day with Jesus.

⁴⁰⁻⁴¹One of the two disciples who heard John's words and began to follow Jesus was a man named Andrew. He went and found his brother, Simon, and told him, "We have found the Anointed One!" (Which is translated, the Christ.) ⁴²Then Andrew brought Simon to meet him. When Jesus gazed upon Andrew's brother, he prophesied to him, "You are Simon and your father's name is John. But from now on you will be called Cephas" (which means, Peter the Rock).

Jesus Calls Philip and Nathanael

⁴³The next day Jesus decided to go to the region of Galilee. There he found Philip and said to him, "Come and follow me." ⁴⁴(Now Philip, Andrew, and Peter were all from the same village of Bethsaida.) ⁴⁵Then Philip went to look for his friend, Nathanael, and told him, "We've found him! We've found the One we've been waiting for! It's Jesus, son of Joseph from Nazareth, the Anointed One! He's the One that Moses and the prophets prophesied would come!"

⁴⁶Nathanael sneered, "Nazareth! What good thing could

ever come from Nazareth?" Philip answered, "Come and let's find out!"

⁴⁷When Jesus saw Nathanael approaching, he said, "Now here comes a true son of Israel—an honest man with no hidden motive!"

⁴⁸Nathanael was stunned and said, "But you've never met me—how do you know anything about me?"

Jesus answered, "Nathanael, right before Philip came to you I saw you sitting under the shade of a fig tree."

⁴⁹Nathanael blurted out, "Teacher, you are truly the Son of God and the King of Israel!"

⁵⁰Jesus answered, "Do you believe simply because I told you I saw you sitting under a fig tree? You will experience even more impressive things than that! ⁵¹I prophesy to you eternal truth: From now on you will see an open heaven and gaze upon the Son of Man like a stairway reaching into the sky with the messengers of God climbing up and down upon him!"

Jesus Comes to a Wedding

2 Now on the third day there was a wedding feast in the Galilean village of Cana, and the mother of Jesus was there. ²⁻³Jesus and his disciples were all invited to the banquet, but with so many guests in attendance, they ran out of wine. And when Mary realized it, she came to him and asked, "They have no wine, can't you do something about it?"

⁴Jesus replied, "My dear one, don't you understand that if I do this, it won't change anything for you, but it will change everything for me! My hour of unveiling my power has not yet come."

⁵Mary then went to the servers and told them, "Whatever Jesus tells you, make sure that you do it!"

⁶Now there were six stone water pots standing nearby. They were meant to be used for the Jewish washing rituals. Each one held about 20 gallons or more. ⁷Jesus came to the servers and told them, "Fill the pots with water, right up to the very brim." ⁸Then he said, "Now fill your pitchers and take them to the master of ceremonies."

⁹And when they poured out their pitcher for the master of ceremonies to sample, the water became wine! When he tasted the water that became wine, the master of ceremonies was impressed. (Although he didn't know where the wine had come from, but the servers knew.) ¹⁰He called the bridegroom over and said to him, "Every host serves his best wine first until everyone has had a cup or two, then he serves the wine of poor quality. But you, my friend, you've reserved the most exquisite wine until now!"

¹¹This miracle in Cana was the first of the many extraordinary miracles Jesus performed in Galilee. This was a sign revealing his glory, and his disciples believed in him.

Jesus at the Temple

¹²After this, Jesus, his mother and brothers and his disciples went to Capernaum and stayed there for a few days. ¹³But the time was close for the Jewish Passover to begin, so Jesus walked to Jerusalem. ¹⁴As he went into the temple courtyard, he noticed it was filled with merchants selling oxen, lambs, and doves for exorbitant prices, while others were overcharging as they exchanged currency behind their

counters. [15]So Jesus found some rope and made it into a whip. Then he drove out every one of them and their animals from the courtyard of the temple, and he kicked over their tables filled with money, scattering it everywhere! [16]And he shouted at the merchants, "Get these things out of here! Don't you dare make my Father's house into a center for merchandise!" [17]That's when his disciples remembered the Scripture: "I am consumed with a fiery passion to keep your house pure!"

[18]But the Jewish religious leaders challenged Jesus, "What authorization do you have to do this sort of thing? If God gave you this kind of authority, what supernatural sign will you show us to prove it?"

[19]Jesus answered, "After you've destroyed this temple, I will raise it up again in three days."

[20]Then the Jewish leaders sneered, "This temple took forty-six years to build, and you mean to tell us that you will raise it up in three days?" [21]But they didn't understand that Jesus was speaking of the "temple" of his body. [22]But the disciples remembered his prophecy after Jesus rose from the dead, and believed both the Scripture and what Jesus had said.

[23]While Jesus was at the Passover Feast, the number of his followers began to grow, and many gave their allegiance to him because of all the miraculous signs they had seen him doing! [24]But Jesus did not yet entrust himself to them, because he knew how fickle human hearts can be. [25]He didn't need anyone to tell him about human nature, for he fully understood what man was capable of doing.

Nicodemus

3 Now there was a prominent religious leader among the Jews named Nicodemus, who was part of the sect called the Pharisees and a member of the Jewish ruling council. ²One night he discreetly came to Jesus and said, "Master, we know that you are a teacher from God, for no one performs the miracle signs that you do, unless God's power is with him."

³Jesus answered, "Nicodemus, listen to this eternal truth: Before a person can perceive God's kingdom realm, they must first experience a rebirth."

⁴Nicodemus said, "Rebirth? How can a gray-headed man be reborn? It's impossible for a man to go back into the womb a second time and be reborn!"

⁵Jesus answered, "I speak an eternal truth: Unless you are born of water and Spirit-wind, you will never enter God's kingdom realm. ⁶For the natural realm can only give birth to things that are natural, but the spiritual realm gives birth to supernatural life!

⁷"You shouldn't be amazed by my statement, 'You must be born from above!' ⁸For the Spirit-wind blows as it chooses. You can hear its sound, but you don't know where it came from or where it's going. So it is within the hearts of those who are Spirit-born!"

⁹Then Nicodemus replied, "But I don't understand, what do you mean? How does this happen?"

¹⁰Jesus answered, "Nicodemus, aren't you the respected teacher in Israel, and yet you don't understand this revelation? ¹¹I speak eternal truths about things I know, things

I've seen and experienced—and still you don't accept what I reveal. [12]If you're unable to understand and believe what I've told you about the natural realm, what will you do when I begin to unveil the heavenly realm? [13]No one has risen into the heavenly realm except the Son of Man who also exists in heaven."

God's Love for Everyone

[14]"And just as Moses in the desert lifted up the brass replica of a snake on a pole for all the people to see and be healed, so the Son of Man is ready to be lifted up, [15]so that those who truly believe in him will not perish but be given eternal life. [16]For this is how much God loved the world—he gave his one and only, unique Son as a gift. So now everyone who believes in him will never perish but experience everlasting life.

[17]"God did not send his Son into the world to judge and condemn the world, but to be its Savior and rescue it! [18]So now there is no longer any condemnation for those who believe in him, but the unbeliever already lives under condemnation because they do not believe in the name of God's beloved Son. [19]And here is the basis for their judgment: The Light of God has now come into the world, but the hearts of people love their darkness more than the Light, because they want the darkness to conceal their evil. [20]So the wicked hate the Light and try to hide from it, for their lives are fully exposed in the Light. [21]But those who love the truth will come out into the Light and welcome its exposure, for the Light will reveal that their fruitful works were produced by God."

John, Friend of the Bridegroom

²²Then Jesus and his disciples went out for a length of time into the Judean countryside where they baptized the people. ²³At this time John was still baptizing people at Aenon, near Salim, where there was plenty of water. And the people kept coming for John to baptize them. ²⁴(This was before John was thrown into prison.)

²⁵An argument then developed between John's disciples and a particular Jewish man about baptism. ²⁶So they went to John and asked him, "Teacher, are you aware that the One you told us about at the crossing place—he's now baptizing everyone with larger crowds than yours. People are flocking to him! What do you think about that?"

²⁷John answered them, "A person cannot receive even one thing unless God bestows it. ²⁸You heard me tell you before that I am not the Messiah, but certainly I am the messenger sent ahead of him. ²⁹He is the Bridegroom, and the bride belongs to him. I am the friend of the Bridegroom who stands nearby and listens with great joy to the Bridegroom's voice. And because of his words my joy is complete and overflows! ³⁰So it's necessary for him to increase and for me to be diminished.

³¹"For the one who is from the earth belongs to the earth and speaks from the natural realm. But the One who comes from above is above everything and speaks of the highest realm of all! ³²His message is about what he has seen and experienced, even though people don't accept it. ³³Yet those who embrace his message know in their hearts that it's the truth.

34"The One whom God has sent to represent him will speak the words of God, for God has poured out upon him the fullness of the Holy Spirit without limitation. 35The Father loves his Son so much that all things have been given into his hands. 36Those who trust in the Son possess eternal life; but those who don't obey the Son will not see life, and God's anger will rise up against them."

A Thirsty Savior

4 Soon the news reached the Jewish religious leaders known as the Pharisees that Jesus was drawing greater crowds of followers coming to be baptized than John. 2(Although Jesus didn't baptize, but had his disciples baptize the people.) 3Jesus heard what was being said and abruptly left Judea and returned to the province of Galilee, 4and he had to pass through Samaritan territory.

5Jesus arrived at the Samaritan village of Sychar, near the field that Jacob had given to his son, Joseph, long ago. 6–8Wearied by his long journey, he sat on the edge of Jacob's well. He sent his disciples into the village to buy food, for it was already afternoon.

Soon a Samaritan woman came to draw water. Jesus said to her, "Give me a drink of water."

9Surprised, she said, "Why would a Jewish man ask a Samaritan woman for a drink of water?"

10Jesus replied, "If you only knew who I am and the gift that God wants to give you—you'd ask me for a drink, and I would give to you living water."

11The woman replied, "But sir, you don't even have a

bucket and this well is very deep. So where do you find this 'living water'? [12]Do you really think that you are greater than our ancestor Jacob who dug this well and drank from it himself, along with his children and livestock?"

[13]Jesus answered, "If you drink from Jacob's well you'll be thirsty again and again, [14]but if anyone drinks the living water I give them, they will never thirst again and will be forever satisfied! For when you drink the water I give you it becomes a gushing fountain of the Holy Spirit, springing up and flooding you with endless life!"

[15]The woman replied, "Let me drink that water so I'll never be thirsty again and won't have to come back here to draw water."

[16]Jesus said, "Go get your husband and bring him back here."

[17]"But I'm not married," the woman answered.

"That's true," Jesus said, [18]"for you've been married five times and now you're living with a man who is not your husband. You have told the truth."

[19]The woman said, "You must be a prophet! [20]So tell me this: Why do our fathers worship God here on this nearby mountain, but your people teach that Jerusalem is the place where we must worship. Which is right?"

Jesus responded, [21]"Believe me, dear woman, the time has come when you won't worship the Father on a mountain nor in Jerusalem, but in your heart. [22]Your people don't really know the One they worship. We Jews worship out of our experience, for it's from the Jews that salvation is made available. [23–24]From here on, worshiping the Father will not be a matter of the right place but with the right heart. For God is a Spirit, and he longs to have sincere worshipers who worship and adore him in the realm of the Spirit and in truth."

25The woman said, "This is all so confusing, but I do know that the Anointed One is coming—the true Messiah. And when he comes, he will tell us everything we need to know."

26Jesus said to her, "You don't have to wait any longer, the Anointed One is here speaking with you—I am the One you're looking for."

27At that moment the disciples returned and were stunned to see Jesus speaking with the Samaritan woman. Yet none of them dared to ask him why or what they were discussing. 28All at once, the woman dropped her water jar and ran off to her village and told everyone, 29"Come and meet a man at the well who told me everything I've ever done! He could be the Anointed One we've been waiting for." 30Hearing this, the people came streaming out of the village to go see Jesus.

The Harvest Is Ready

31Then the disciples began to insist that Jesus eat some of the food they brought back from the village, saying, "Teacher, you must eat something." 32But Jesus told them, "Don't worry about me. I have eaten a meal you don't know about."

33Puzzled by this, the disciples began to discuss among themselves, "Did someone already bring him food? Where did he get this meal?"

34Then Jesus spoke up and said, "My food is to be doing the will of him who sent me and bring it to completion."

³⁵As the crowds emerged from the village, Jesus said to his disciples, "Why would you say, 'The harvest is another four months away'? Look at all the people coming—now is harvest time! For their hearts are like vast fields of ripened grain—ready for a spiritual harvest. ³⁶And everyone who reaps these souls for eternal life will receive a reward. And those who plant spiritual seeds and those who reap the harvest will celebrate together with great joy! ³⁷And this confirms the saying, 'One sows the seed and another reaps the harvest.' ³⁸I have sent you out to harvest a field that you haven't planted, where many others have labored long and hard before you. And now you are privileged to profit from their labors and reap the harvest."

³⁹So there were many from the Samaritan village who became believers in Jesus because of the woman's testimony: "He told me everything I ever did!" ⁴⁰Then they begged Jesus to stay with them, so he stayed there for two days, ⁴¹resulting in many more coming to faith in him because of his teachings.

⁴²Then the Samaritans said to the woman, "We no longer believe just because of what you told us, but now we've heard him ourselves and are convinced that he really is the true Savior of the world!"

Jesus Returns to Galilee

⁴³On the third day Jesus left there and walked to the province of Galilee, where he was raised. ⁴⁴Now Jesus knew that prophets are honored everywhere they go except in their own hometown. ⁴⁵Even so, as Jesus arrived in the province of Gal-

ilee, he was welcomed by the people with open arms. Many of them had been in Jerusalem during the Passover Festival and had witnessed firsthand the miracles he had performed.

46–47 Jesus entered the village of Cana of Galilee where he had transformed water into wine. And there was a governmental official in Capernaum who had a son who was very sick and dying. When he heard that Jesus had left Judea and was staying in Cana of Galilee, he decided to make the journey to Cana. When he found Jesus he begged him, "You must come with me to Capernaum and heal my son!"

48 So Jesus said to him, "You never believe unless you see signs and wonders."

49 But the man continued to plead, "You have to come with me to Capernaum before my little boy dies!"

50 Then Jesus looked him in the eyes and said, "Go back home now. I promise you, your son will live and not die."

The man believed in his heart the words of Jesus and set off for home. 51 When he was still a distance from Capernaum, his servants met him on the road and told him the good news, "Your son is healed! He's alive!"

52 Overjoyed, the father asked his servants, "When did my son begin to recover?"

"Yesterday," they said, "at one in the afternoon. All at once his fever broke—and now he's well!"

53 Then the father realized that it was at that very same hour that Jesus spoke the words to him, "Your son will live and not die." So from that day forward, the man and all his family and servants believed. 54 This was Jesus' second extraordinary miracle in Galilee after coming from Judea.

The Healing at Bethesda

5 Then Jesus returned to Jerusalem to observe one of the Jewish holy days. ²Inside the city near the Sheep Gate there is a pool called in Aramaic, The House of Loving Kindness. And this pool is surrounded by five covered porches. ³Hundreds of sick people were lying there on the porches—the paralyzed, the blind, and the crippled, all of them waiting for their healing. ⁴For an angel of God would periodically descend into the pool to stir the waters, and the first one who stepped into the pool after the waters swirled would instantly be healed.

⁵Now there was a man who had been disabled for thirty-eight years lying among the multitude of the sick. ⁶When Jesus saw him lying there, he knew that the man had been crippled for a long time. So Jesus said to him, "Do you truly long to be healed?"

⁷The sick man answered him, "Sir, there's no way I can get healed, for I have no one who will lower me into the water when the angel comes. As soon as I try to crawl to the edge of the pool, someone else jumps in ahead of me."

⁸Then Jesus said to him, "Stand up! Pick up your sleeping mat and you will walk!" ⁹Immediately he stood up—he was healed! So he rolled up his mat and walked again! Now this miracle took place on the Jewish Sabbath.

¹⁰When the Jewish leaders saw the man walking along carrying his sleeping mat, they objected and said, "What are you doing carrying that? Don't you know it's the Sabbath? It's not lawful for you to carry things on the Sabbath!"

¹¹He answered them, "The man who healed me told me to pick it up and walk."

¹²"What man?" they asked him. "Who was this man who ordered you to carry something on a Sabbath?" ¹³But the healed man couldn't give them an answer, for he didn't yet know who it was since Jesus had already slipped away into the crowd.

¹⁴A short time later, Jesus found the man at the temple and said to him, "Look at you now! You're healed! Walk away from your sin so that nothing worse will happen to you."

¹⁵Then the man went to the Jewish leaders to inform them, "It was Jesus who healed me!" ¹⁶So from that day forward the Jewish leaders began to persecute Jesus because of the things he did on the Sabbath.

Jesus Responds to the Jewish Leaders

¹⁷Jesus answered his critics by saying, "Everyday my Father is at work, and I will be too!" ¹⁸This infuriated them and made them all the more eager to devise a plan to kill him. For not only did he break their Sabbath rules, but he called God "my Father," which made him equal to God.

¹⁹So Jesus said, "I speak to you timeless truth. The Son is not able to do anything from himself or through my own initiative. I only do the works that I see the Father doing, for the Son does the same works as his Father.

²⁰"Because the Father loves his Son so much, he always reveals to me everything that he is about to do. And you will all be amazed when he shows me even greater works than what you've seen so far! ²¹For just like the Father has power to raise the dead, the Son will raise the dead and give life to whomever he wants.

²²"The Father now judges no one, for he has given all the authority to judge to the Son, ²³so that the honor that belongs to the Father will now be shared with his Son. So if you refuse to honor the Son, you are refusing to honor the Father who sent him.

²⁴"I speak to you an eternal truth: if you embrace my message and believe in the One who sent me, you will never face condemnation, for in me, you have already passed from the realm of death into the realm of eternal life!"

Two Resurrections

²⁵"I speak to you eternal truth: Soon the dead will hear the voice of the Son of God, and those who listen will arise with life! ²⁶For the Father has given the Son the power to impart life, even as the Father imparts life. ²⁷The Father has transferred to the Son the authority to judge, because he is the Son of Man.

²⁸"So don't be amazed when I tell you these things, for there is a day coming when all who have ever died will hear my voice calling them back to life, ²⁹and they will come out of their graves! Those who have done what is good will experience a resurrection to eternal life. And those who have practiced evil will taste the resurrection that brings them to condemnation!

³⁰"Nothing I do is from my own initiative, for as I hear the judgment passed by my Father, I execute judgment. And my judgments will be perfect, because I can do nothing on my own, except to fulfill the desires of my Father who sent me. ³¹For if I were to make claims about myself, you would have

reasons to doubt. [32]But there is another who bears witness on my behalf, and I know that what he testifies of me is true."

John the Baptizer

[33]"You have sent messengers to John, and what he testified about me is true. [34]I have no need to be validated by men, but I'm saying these things so that you will believe and be rescued.

[35]"John was a blazing, burning torch, and for a short time you basked in his light with great joy. [36]But I can provide a more substantial proof of who I am that exceeds John's testimony—my miracles! These works which the Father destined for me to complete—they prove that the Father has sent me! [37]And my Father himself, who gave me this mission, has also testified that I am his Son. But you have never heard his voice nor seen his face, [38]nor does his Word truly live inside of you, for you refuse to believe in me or to embrace me as God's messenger.

[39]"You are busy analyzing the Scriptures, frantically poring over them in hopes of gaining eternal life. Everything you read points to me, [40]yet you still refuse to come to me so I can give you the life you're looking for—eternal life!

[41]"I do not accept the honor that comes from men, [42]for I know what kind of people you really are, and I can see that the love of God has found no home in you. [43]I have come to represent my Father, yet you refuse to embrace me in faith. But when someone comes in their own name and with their own agenda, you readily accept him. [44]Of course you're unable to believe in me. For you live for the praises of others and not for the praise that comes from the only true God.

⁴⁵"I won't be the one who accuses you before the Father. The one who will incriminate you is Moses, the very one you claim to obey, the one in whom you trust! ⁴⁶If you really believed what Moses has written, then you would embrace me, for Moses wrote about me! ⁴⁷But since you do not believe what he wrote, no wonder you don't believe what I say."

Jesus Multiplies Food

6 After this Jesus went to the other side of the Lake of Tiberias, which is also known as Lake Galilee. ²And a massive crowd of people followed him everywhere. They were attracted by his miracles and the healings they watched him perform. ³Jesus went up the slope of a hill and sat down with his disciples. ⁴Now it was approaching the time of the Jewish celebration of Passover, and there were many pilgrims on their way to Jerusalem in the crowd.

⁵As Jesus sat down, he looked out and saw the massive crowd of people scrambling up the hill, for they wanted to be near him. So he turned to Philip and said, "Where will we buy enough food to feed all these people?" ⁶Now Jesus already knew what he was about to do, but he said this to stretch Philip's faith.

⁷Philip answered, "Well, I suppose if we were to give everyone only a snack, it would cost thousands of dollars to buy enough food!"

⁸But just then, Andrew, Peter's brother, spoke up and said, ⁹"Look! Here's a young person with five barley loaves and two small fish . . . but how far would that go with this huge crowd?"

[10]"Have everyone sit down," Jesus said to his disciples. So on the vast grassy slope, more than five thousand hungry people sat down. [11]Jesus then took the barley loaves and the fish and gave thanks to God. He then gave it to the disciples to distribute to the people. Miraculously, the food multiplied, with everyone eating as much as they wanted!

[12]When everyone was satisfied, Jesus told his disciples, "Now go back and gather up the pieces left over so that nothing will be wasted." [13]The disciples filled up twelve baskets of fragments, a basket of leftovers for each disciple.

[14]All the people were astounded as they saw with their own eyes the incredible miracle Jesus had performed! They began to say among themselves, "He really is the One—the true prophet we've been expecting!"

[15]So Jesus, knowing that they were about to take him and make him their king by force, quickly left and went up the mountainside alone.

Jesus Walks on Water

[16–17]After waiting until evening for Jesus to return, the disciples went down to the lake. But as darkness fell, he still hadn't returned, so the disciples got into a boat and headed across the lake to Capernaum. [18]By now a strong wind began to blow and was stirring up the waters. [19]The disciples had rowed about halfway across the lake when all of a sudden they caught sight of Jesus walking on top of the waves, coming toward them. The disciples panicked, [20]but Jesus called out to them, "Don't be afraid. You know who I am."

[21]They were relieved to take him in, and the moment Jesus

stepped into the boat, they were instantly transported to the other side!

Jesus, the Living Bread

22-23The next morning, the crowds were still on the opposite shore of the lake, near the place where they had eaten the bread he had multiplied after he had given thanks to God. Yet Jesus was nowhere to be found. They realized that only one boat had been there and that Jesus' hadn't boarded, and they concluded that his disciples had left him behind. 24So when the people saw on the shoreline a number of small boats from Tiberias and realized Jesus and the disciples weren't there, they got into the boats and went to Capernaum to search for him.

25When they finally found him, they asked him, "Teacher, how did you get here?"

26Jesus replied, "Let me make this very clear, you came looking for me because I fed you by a miracle, not because you believe in me. 27Why would you strive for food that is perishable and not be passionate to seek the food of eternal life, which never spoils? I, the Son of Man, am ready to give you what matters most, for God the Father has destined me for this purpose."

28They replied, "So what should we do if we want to do God's work?"

29Jesus answered, "The work you can do for God starts with believing in the One he has sent."

30-31They replied, "Show us a miracle so we can see it, and then we'll believe in you. Moses took care of our ancestors who were fed by the miracle of manna every day in the desert, just like the Scripture says, 'He fed them with bread from heaven.' What sign will you perform for us?"

[32]"The truth is," Jesus said, "Moses didn't give you the bread of heaven. It's my Father who offers bread that comes as a dramatic sign from heaven. [33]The bread of God is the One who came out of heaven to give his life to feed the world."

[34]"Then please, sir, give us this bread every day," they replied.

[35]Jesus said to them, "I am the Bread of Life. Come every day to me and you will never be hungry. Believe in me and you will never be thirsty. [36]Yet I've told you that even though you've seen me, you still don't believe in me. [37]But everyone my Father has given to me, they will come. And all who come to me, I will embrace and will never turn them away. [38]And I have come out of heaven not for my own desires, but for the satisfaction of my Father who sent me. [39]My Father who sent me has determined that I will not lose even one of those he has given to me, and I will raise them up in the last day. [40]For the longing of my Father is that everyone who embraces the Son and believes in him will experience eternal life and I will raise them up in the last day!"

[41]When the Jews who were hostile to Jesus heard him say, "I am the bread that came down from heaven," they immediately began to complain, [42]"How can he say these things about himself? We know him, and we know his parents. How dare he say, 'I have come down from heaven?'"

[43]Jesus responded, "Stop your grumbling! [44]The only way

people come to me is by the Father who sent me—he pulls on their hearts to embrace me. And those who are drawn to me, I will certainly raise them up in the last day."

45 Jesus continued, "It has been written by the prophets, 'They will all be taught by God himself.' If you are really listening to the Father and learning directly from him, you will come to me. 46For I am the only One who has come from the Father's side, and I have seen the Father!

47"I speak to you living truth: Unite your heart to me and believe—and you will experience eternal life! 48I am the true Bread of Life. 49Your ancestors ate manna in the desert and died. 50But standing here before you is the true Bread that comes out of heaven, and when you eat this Bread you will never die. 51I alone am this living Bread that has come to you from heaven. Eat this Bread and you will live forever. The living Bread I give you is my body, which I will offer as a sacrifice so that all may live."

52These words of Jesus sparked an angry outburst among the Jews. They protested, saying, "Does this man expect us to eat his body?"

53 Jesus replied to them, "Listen to this eternal truth: Unless you eat the body of the Son of Man and drink his blood, you will not have eternal life. 54Eternal life comes to the one who eats my body and drinks my blood, and I will raise him up in the last day. 55For my body is real food for your spirit and my blood is real drink. 56The one who eats my body and drinks my blood lives in me and I live in him. 57The Father of life sent me, and he is my life. In the same way, the one who feeds upon me, I will become his life. 58I am not like the bread your

ancestors ate and later died. I am the living Bread that comes from heaven. Eat this Bread and you will live forever!"

59 Jesus preached this sermon in the synagogue in Capernaum.

Many Disciples Became Offended

60 And when many of Jesus' followers heard these things, it caused a stir. "That's disgusting!" they said. "How could anybody accept it?"

61 Without anyone telling him, Jesus knew they were outraged and told them, "Are you offended over my teaching? 62 What will you do when you see the Son of Man ascending into the realm from where he came?

63 "The Holy Spirit is the one who gives life, that which is of the natural realm is of no help. The words I speak to you are Spirit and life. But there are still some of you who won't believe." 64 In fact, Jesus already knew from the beginning who the skeptics were and who his traitor would be.

65 He went on to say, "This is why I told you that no one embraces me unless the Father has given you to me."

Peter's Confession of Faith

66 And so from that time on many of the disciples turned their backs on Jesus and refused to be associated with him. 67 So Jesus said to his twelve, "And you—do you also want to leave?" 68 Peter spoke up and said, "But Lord, where would we go? No one but you gives us the revelation of eternal life. 69 We're fully convinced that you are the Anointed One, the Son of the Living God, and we believe in you!"

⁷⁰Then Jesus shocked them with these words: "I have hand-picked you to be my twelve, knowing that one of you is the devil." ⁷¹Jesus was referring to Judas Iscariot, son of Simon, for he knew that Judas, one of his chosen disciples, was getting ready to betray him.

Jesus at the Feast of Tabernacles

7After this Jesus traveled extensively throughout the province of Galilee, but he avoided the province of Judea, for he knew the Jewish leaders in Jerusalem were plotting to have him killed. ²Now the annual Feast of Tabernacles was approaching. ³So Jesus' brothers came to advise him, saying, "Why don't you leave the countryside villages and go to Judea where the crowds are, so that your followers can see your miracles? ⁴No one can see what you're doing here in the backwoods of Galilee. How do you expect to be successful and famous if you do all these things in secret? Now is your time—go to Jerusalem, come out of hiding, and show the world who you are!" ⁵His brothers were pushing him, even though they didn't yet believe in him as the Savior.

⁶Jesus responded, "My time of being unveiled hasn't yet come, but any time is a suitable opportunity for you to gain man's approval. ⁷The world can't hate you, but it does me, for I am exposing their evil deeds. ⁸You can go ahead and celebrate the feast without me—my appointed time has not yet come."

⁹⁻¹⁰Jesus lingered in Galilee until his brothers had left for the feast in Jerusalem. Then later, Jesus took a back road and went into Jerusalem in secret. ¹¹During the feast, the Jewish

leaders kept looking for Jesus and asking around, "Where is he? Have you seen him?"

¹²A controversy was brewing among the people, with so many differing opinions about Jesus. Some were saying, "He's a good man!" While others weren't convinced and insisted, saying, "He's just a demagogue." ¹³Yet no one was bold enough to speak out publicly on Jesus' behalf for fear of the Jewish leaders.

¹⁴Not until the feast was half over did Jesus finally appear in the temple courts and begin to teach. ¹⁵The Jewish leaders were astonished by what he taught and said, "How did this man acquire such knowledge? He wasn't trained in our schools—who taught him?"

¹⁶So Jesus responded, "I don't teach my own ideas, but the truth revealed to me by the One who sent me. ¹⁷If you want to test my teachings and discover where I received them, first be passionate to do God's will, and then you will be able to discern if my teachings are from the heart of God or from my own opinions. ¹⁸Charlatans praise themselves and seek honor from men, but my Father sent me to speak truth on his behalf. And I have no false motive, because I seek only the glory of God. ¹⁹Moses has given you the law, but not one of you is faithful to keep it. So if you are all law-breakers, why then would you seek to kill me?"

²⁰Then some in the crowd shouted out, "You must be out of your mind! Who's trying to kill you?"

²¹Jesus replied, "I only had to do one miracle, and all of you marvel! ²²Yet isn't it true that Moses and your forefathers ordered you to circumcise your sons even if the eighth day fell

on a Sabbath? 23So if you cut away part of a man on the Sabbath and that doesn't break the Jewish law, why then would you be indignant with me for making a man completely healed on the Sabbath? 24Stop judging based on the superficial. First you must embrace the standards of mercy and truth."

25Then some of the residents of Jerusalem spoke up and said, "Isn't this the one they're trying to kill? 26So why is he here speaking publicly and not one of the Jewish leaders is doing anything about it? Are they starting to think that he's the Anointed One? 27But how could he be, since we know this man is from Galilee, but no one will know where the true Messiah comes from, he'll just appear out of nowhere."

28Knowing all of this, Jesus one day preached boldly in the temple courts, "So, you think you know me and where I come from? But you don't know the One who sent me—the Father who is always faithful. I have not come simply on my own initiative. 29The Father has sent me here, and I know all about him, for I have come from his presence."

30His words caused many to want to arrest him, but no man was able to lay a hand on him, for it wasn't yet his appointed time. 31And there were many people who thought he might be the Messiah. They said, "After all, when the Anointed One appears, could he possibly do more signs and wonders than this man has done?"

32So when the Pharisees heard these rumors circulating about Jesus, they went with the leading priests and the temple guards to arrest him.

33Then Jesus said, "My days to be with you are numbered. Then I will return to the One who sent me. 34And you will search for me and not be able to find me. For where I am, you cannot come."

35When the Jewish leaders heard this, they discussed among themselves, "Where could he possibly go that we won't be able to find him? Is he going to minister in a different land where our people live scattered among the nations? Is he going to teach those who are not Jews? 36What did he really mean by his statement, 'You will search for me and won't be able to find me. And where I am you can't come'?"

Rivers of Living Water

37Then on the most important day of the feast, the last day, Jesus stood and shouted out to the crowds—"All you thirsty ones, come to me! Come to me and drink! 38Believe in me so that rivers of living water will burst out from within you, flowing from your innermost being, just like the Scripture says!"

39Jesus was prophesying about the Holy Spirit that believers were being prepared to receive. But the Holy Spirit had not yet been poured out upon them, because Jesus had not yet been unveiled in his full splendor.

Divided Opinions about Jesus

40When the crowd heard Jesus' words, some said, "This man really is a prophet!" 41Others said, "He's the Messiah!" But others said, "How could he be the Anointed One since he's from Galilee? 42Don't the Scriptures say that he will be one of David's descendants and be born in Bethlehem, the city of David?" 43So the crowd was divided over Jesus, 44some wanted him arrested but no one dared to lay a hand on him.

The Unbelief of Religious Leaders

⁴⁵So when the temple guards returned to the Pharisees and the leading priests without Jesus, they were questioned, "Where is he? Why didn't you bring that man back with you?"

⁴⁶They answered, "You don't understand—he speaks amazing things like no one else has ever spoken!"

⁴⁷The religious leaders mocked, "Oh, so now you also have been led astray by him? ⁴⁸Do you see even one of us, your leaders, following him? ⁴⁹This ignorant rabble swarms around him because none of them know anything about the Law! They're all cursed!"

⁵⁰Just then, Nicodemus, who had secretly spent time with Jesus, spoke up, for he was a respected voice among them. ⁵¹He cautioned them, saying, "Does our law decide a man's guilt before we first hear him and allow him to defend himself?"

⁵²They argued, "Oh, so now you're an advocate for this Galilean! Search the Scriptures, Nicodemus, and you'll see that there's no mention of a prophet coming out of Galilee!" So with that their debate ended, ⁵³and they each went their own way.

An Adulteress Forgiven

8 Jesus walked up the Mount of Olives near the city where he spent the night. ²Then at dawn Jesus appeared in the temple courts again, and soon all the people gathered around to listen to his words, so he sat down and taught them. ³Then in the middle of his teaching, the religious scholars and the Pharisees broke through the crowd and brought

a woman who had been caught in the act of committing adultery and made her stand in the middle of everyone.

4Then they said to Jesus, "Teacher, we caught this woman in the very act of adultery. 5Doesn't Moses' law command us to stone to death a woman like this? Tell us, what do you say we should do with her?" 6They were only testing Jesus because they hoped to trap him with his own words and accuse him of breaking the laws of Moses.

But Jesus didn't answer them. Instead he simply bent down and wrote in the dust with his finger. 7Angry, they kept insisting that he answer their question, so Jesus stood up and looked at them and said, "Let's have the man who has never had a sinful desire throw the first stone at her." 8And then he bent over again and wrote some more words in the dust.

9Upon hearing that, her accusers slowly left the crowd one at a time, beginning with the oldest to the youngest, with a convicted conscience. 10Until finally, Jesus was left alone with the woman still standing there in front of him. So he stood back up and said to her, "Dear woman, where are your accusers? Is there no one here to condemn you?"

11Looking around, she replied, "I see no one, Lord."

Jesus said, "Then I certainly don't condemn you either. Go, and from now on, be free from a life of sin."

Jesus, the Light of the World

12Then Jesus said, "I am light to the world and those who embrace me will experience life-giving light, and they will never walk in darkness."

13The Pharisees were immediately offended and said,

"You're just boasting about yourself! Since we only have your word on this, it makes your testimony invalid!"

¹⁴Jesus responded, "Just because I am the one making these claims doesn't mean they're invalid. For I absolutely know who I am, where I've come from, and where I'm going. But you Pharisees have no idea about what I'm saying. ¹⁵For you've set yourselves up as judges of others based on outward appearances, but I certainly never judge others in that way. ¹⁶For I discern the truth. And I am not alone in my judgments, for my Father and I have the same understanding in all things, and he has sent me to you.

¹⁷"Isn't it written in the law of Moses that the testimony of two men is trustworthy? ¹⁸Then what I say about who I am is true, for I am not alone in my testimony—my Father is the other witness, and we testify together of the truth."

¹⁹Then they asked, "Just who is this 'Father' of yours? Where is he?"

Jesus answered, "You wouldn't ask that question if you knew who I am, or my Father. For if you knew me, you would recognize my Father too." ²⁰(Jesus taught all these things while standing in the treasure room of the temple. And no one dared to arrest him, for it wasn't yet his time to surrender to men.)

"I Am Not from This World"

²¹One day Jesus said again, "I am about to leave you. You will want to find me, but you will still die in your sins. You won't be able to come where I am going."

²²This so confused the Jewish leaders that they began to

say, "Is he planning to commit suicide? What's he talking about—'You won't be able to come where I am going'?"

23 Jesus spoke up and said, "You are all from the earth; I am from above. I am not from this world like you are. 24 That's why I've told you that you will all die in your sins if you fail to believe that I AM who I AM."

25 So they asked him plainly, "Who are you?"

"I am the One I've always claimed to be." Jesus replied. 26 "And I still have many more things to pronounce in judgment about you. For I will testify to the world of the truths that I have heard from my Father, and the Father who sent me is trustworthy." 27 (Even after all of this, they still didn't realize that he was speaking about his heavenly Father.)

28 "You will know me as 'I AM' after you have lifted me up from the earth as the Son of Man. Then you will realize that I do nothing on my own initiative, but I only speak the truth that the Father has revealed to me. 29 I am his messenger and he is always with me, for I only do that which delights his heart." 30 These words caused many respected Jews to believe in him.

The Son Gives Freedom

31 Jesus said to those Jews who believed in him, "When you continue to embrace all that I teach, you prove that you are my true followers. 32 For if you embrace the truth, it will release more freedom into your lives."

33 Surprised by this, they said, "But we're the descendants of Abraham and we're already free. We've never been in bondage to anyone. How could you say that we will be released into more freedom?"

³⁴"I speak eternal truth," Jesus said. "When you sin you are not free. You've become a slave in bondage to your sin. ³⁵And slaves have no permanent standing in a family, like a son does, for a son is a part of the family forever. ³⁶So if the Son sets you free from sin, then become a true son and be unquestionably free! ³⁷Even though you are descendants of Abraham, you desire to kill me because the message I bring has not found a home in your hearts. ³⁸Yet the truths I speak I've seen and received in my Father's presence. But you are doing what you've learned from your father!"

³⁹"What do mean?" they replied. "Abraham is our father!"

Jesus said, "If you are really Abraham's sons, then you would follow in the steps of Abraham. ⁴⁰I've only told you the truth that I've heard in my Father's presence, but now you are wanting me dead—is that how Abraham acted? ⁴¹No, you people are doing what your father has taught you!"

Indignant, they responded, "What are you talking about? We only have one Father, God himself! We're not illegitimate!"

⁴²Jesus said, "Then if God were really your father, you would love me, for I've come from his presence. I didn't come here on my own, but God sent me to you. ⁴³Why don't you understand what I say? You don't understand because your hearts are closed to my message!

⁴⁴"You are the offspring of your father, the devil, and you serve your father very well, passionately carrying out his desires. He's been a murderer right from the start! He never stood with the One who is the true Prince, for he's full of nothing but lies—lying is his native tongue. He is a master of

deception and the father of lies! 45But I am the true Prince who speaks nothing but the truth, yet you refuse to believe and you want nothing to do with me. 46Can you name one sin that I've committed? Then if I am telling you only the truth, why don't you believe me? 47If you really knew God, you would listen, receive, and respond with faith to his words. But since you don't listen and respond to what he says, it proves you don't belong to him and you have no room for him in your hearts."

48"See! We were right all along!" some of the Jewish leaders shouted. "You're nothing but a demon-possessed Samaritan!"

49Jesus replied, "It is not a demon that would cause me to honor my Father. I live my life for his honor, even though you insult me for it. 50I never have a need to seek my own glory, for the Father will do that for me, and he will judge those who do not. 51I speak to you this eternal truth: whoever cherishes my words and keeps them will never experience death."

52This prompted the Jewish leaders to say, "Now we know for sure that you're demon possessed! You just said that those who keep watch over your words will never experience death, but Abraham and all the prophets have died! 53Do you think you're greater than our father Abraham and all the prophets? You are so delusional about yourself that you make yourself greater than you are!"

54Jesus answered them, "If I were to tell you how great I am, it would mean nothing. But my Father is the One who will prove it and will glorify me. Isn't he the One you claim is your God? 55But in reality, you've never embraced him as your own. I know him, and I would be a liar, like yourselves, if I told you anything less than that. I have fully embraced him, and I treasure his every word. 56And not only that, Abraham, your ancestor, was overjoyed when he received the revelation of my coming to earth. Yes, he foresaw me coming and was filled with delight!"

57But many of the Jewish leaders doubted him and said, "What are you talking about? You're not even fifty years old yet. You talk like you've seen Abraham!"

58Jesus said to them, "I give you this eternal truth: I have existed long before Abraham was born, for I AM!"

59When they heard this, they picked up rocks to stone him, but Jesus concealed himself as he passed through the crowd and went away from there.

Jesus Healed a Man Born Blind

9 Afterward, as Jesus walked down the street, he noticed a man blind from birth. 2His disciples asked him, "Teacher, whose sin caused this guy's blindness, his own, or the sin of his parents?"

3Jesus answered, "Neither. It happened to him so that you could watch him experience God's miracle. 4While I am with you, it is daytime and we must do the works of God who sent me while the light shines. For there is coming a dark night when no one will be able to work. 5As long as I am with you my life is the light that pierces the world's darkness."

6Then Jesus spat on the ground and made some clay with his saliva. Then he anointed the blind man's eyes with the clay. 7And he said to the blind man, "Now go and wash the clay from your eyes in the ritual pool of Siloam." So he went and washed his face and as he came back, he could see for the first time in his life!

8This caused quite a stir among the people of the neighborhood, for they noticed the blind beggar was now seeing! They began to say to one another, "Isn't this the blind man who once sat and begged?" 9Some said, "No, it can't be him!" Others said, "But it looks just like him—it has to be him!" All the while the man kept insisting, "I'm the man who was blind!"

10Finally, they asked him, "What has happened to you?"

11He replied, "I met the man named Jesus! He rubbed clay on my eyes and said, 'Go to the pool named Siloam and wash.' So I went and while I was washing the clay from my eyes I began to see for the very first time ever!"

12So the people of the neighborhood inquired, "Where is this man?"

"I have no idea." the man replied.

13So the people marched him over to the Pharisees to speak with them. 14They were concerned because the miracle Jesus performed by making clay with his saliva and anointing the man's eyes happened on a Sabbath day, a day that no one was allowed to "work."

15Then the Pharisees asked the man, "How did you have your sight restored?"

He replied, "A man anointed my eyes with clay, then I washed, and now I can see for the first time in my life!"

16Then an argument broke out among the Pharisees over the healing of the blind man on the Sabbath. Some said, "This man who performed this healing is clearly not from

God! He doesn't even observe the Sabbath!" Others said, "If Jesus is just an ordinary sinner, how could he perform a miracle like that?"

¹⁷This prompted them to turn on the man healed of blindness, putting him on the spot in front of them all, demanding an answer. They asked, "Who do you say he is—this man who opened your blind eyes?"

"He's a prophet of God!" the man replied.

¹⁸Still refusing to believe that the man had been healed and was truly blind from birth, the Jewish leaders called for the man's parents to be brought to them.

^{19–20}So they asked his parents, "Is this your son?"

"Yes," they answered.

"Was he really born blind?"

"Yes, he was," they replied.

So they pressed his parents to answer, "Then how is it that he's now seeing?"

²¹"We have no idea," they answered. "We don't know what happened to our son. Ask him, he's a mature adult. He can speak for himself." ²²(Now the parents were obviously intimidated by the Jewish religious leaders, for they had already announced to the people that if anyone publicly confessed Jesus as the Messiah, they would be excommunicated. ²³That's why they told them, "Ask him, he's a mature adult. He can speak for himself.")

²⁴So once again they summoned the man who was healed of blindness and said to him, "Swear to God to tell us the truth! We know the man who healed you is a sinful man! Do you agree?"

²⁵The healed man replied, "I have no idea what kind of man he is. All I know is that I was blind and now I can see for the first time in my life!"

²⁶"But what did he do to you?" they asked. "How did he heal you?"

²⁷The man responded, "I told you once and you didn't listen to me. Why do you make me repeat it? Are you wanting to be his followers too?"

²⁸This angered the Jewish leaders. They heaped insults on him, "We can tell you are one of his followers—now we know it! We are true followers of Moses, ²⁹for we know that God spoke to Moses directly. But as for this one, we don't know where he's coming from!"

³⁰"Well, what a surprise this is!" the man said. "You don't even know where he comes from, but he healed my eyes and now I can see! ³¹We know that God doesn't listen to sinners, but only to godly people who do his will. ³²Yet who has ever heard of a man born blind that was healed and given back his eyesight? ³³I tell you, if this man isn't from God, he wouldn't be able to heal me like he has!"

³⁴Some of the Jewish leaders were enraged and said, "Just who do you think you are to lecture us! You were born a blind, filthy sinner!" So they threw the man out in the street.

³⁵When Jesus learned they had thrown him out, he went to find him and said to him, "Do you believe in the Son of God?"

³⁶The man whose blind eyes were healed answered, "Who is he, Master? Tell me so that I can place all my faith in him."

³⁷Jesus replied, "You're looking right at him. He's speaking with you. It's me, the one in front of you now."

³⁸Then the man threw himself at his feet and worshiped Jesus and said, "Lord, I believe in you!"

³⁹And Jesus said, "I have come to judge those who think they see and make them blind. And for those who are blind, I have come to make them see."

⁴⁰Some of the Pharisees were standing nearby and over-heard these words. They interrupted Jesus and said, "You mean to tell us that we are blind?"

⁴¹Jesus told them, "If you would acknowledge your blindness, then your sin would be removed. But now that you claim to see, your sin remains with you!"

The Parable of the Kind Shepherd

10 Jesus said to the Pharisees, "Listen to this eternal truth: The person who sneaks over the wall to enter into the sheep pen, rather than coming through the gate, reveals himself as a thief coming to steal. ²But the true Shepherd walks right up to the gate, ³and because the gatekeeper knows who he is, he opens the gate to let him in. And the sheep recognize the voice of the true Shepherd, for he calls his own by name and leads them out, for they belong to him. ⁴And when he has brought out all his sheep, he walks ahead of them and they will follow him, for they are familiar with his voice. ⁵But they will run away from strangers and never follow them because they know it's the voice of a stranger." ⁶Jesus told the Pharisees this parable even though they didn't understand a word of what he meant.

⁷So Jesus went over it again, "I speak to you eternal truth: I am the Gate for the flock. ⁸All those who broke in before

me are thieves who came to steal, but the sheep never listened to them. ⁹I am the Gateway. To enter through me is to experience life, freedom, and satisfaction. ¹⁰A thief has only one thing in mind—he wants to steal, slaughter, and destroy. But I have come to give you everything in abundance, more than you expect—life in its fullness until you overflow! ¹¹I am the Good Shepherd who lays down my life as a sacrifice for the sheep. ¹²⁻¹³But the worker who serves only for wages is not a real shepherd. Because he has no heart for the sheep he will run away and abandon them when he sees the wolf coming. And then the wolf mauls the sheep, drags them off, and scatters them.

¹⁴"I alone am the Good Shepherd, and I know those whose hearts are mine, for they recognize me and know me, ¹⁵just as my Father knows my heart and I know my Father's heart. I am ready to give my life for the sheep.

¹⁶"And I have other sheep that I will gather which are not of this Jewish flock. And I, their shepherd, must lead them too, and they will follow me and listen to my voice. And I will join them all into one flock with one shepherd.

¹⁷"The Father has an intense love for me because I freely give my own life—to raise it up again. ¹⁸I surrender my own life, and no one has the power to take my life from me. I have the authority to lay it down and the power to take it back again. This is the destiny my Father has set before me."

¹⁹This teaching set off another heated controversy among the Jewish leaders. ²⁰Many of them said, "This man is a demon-possessed lunatic! Why would anyone listen to a word he says?" ²¹But then there were others who weren't so sure: "His teach-

ing is full of insight. These are not the ravings of a madman! How could a demonized man give sight to one born blind?"

Jesus at the Feast of Renewal

22-23The time came to observe the winter Feast of Renewal in Jerusalem. Jesus walked into the temple area under Solomon's covered walkway 24when the Jewish leaders encircled him and said, "How much longer will you keep us in suspense? Tell us the truth and clarify this for us once and for all. Are you really the Messiah, the Anointed One?"

25Jesus answered them, "I have told you the truth already and you did not believe me. The proof of who I am is revealed by all the miracles that I do in the name of my Father. 26Yet, you stubbornly refuse to follow me, because you are not my sheep. As I've told you before: 27My own sheep will hear my voice and I know each one, and they will follow me. 28I give to them the gift of eternal life and they will never be lost and no one has the power to snatch them out of my hands. 29My Father, who has given them to me as his gift, is the mightiest of all, and no one has the power to snatch them from my Father's care. 30The Father and I are one."

31When they heard this, the Jewish leaders were so enraged that they picked up rocks to stone him to death. 32But Jesus said, "My Father has empowered me to work many miracles and acts of mercy among you. So which one of them do you want to stone me for?"

33The Jewish leaders responded, "We're not stoning you for anything good you did—it's because of your blasphemy! You're just a son of Adam, but you've claimed to be God!"

[34]Jesus answered, "Isn't it written in your Scriptures that God said, 'You are gods?' The Scriptures cannot be denied or found to be in error. [35]So if those who have the message of the Scriptures are said to be 'gods,' then why would you accuse me of blasphemy? [36]For I have been uniquely chosen by God and he is the one who sent me to you. How then could it be blasphemy for me to say, 'I am the Son of God!' [37]If I'm not doing the beautiful works that my Father sent me to do, then don't believe me. [38]But if you see me doing the beautiful works of God upon the earth, then you should at least believe the evidence of the miracles, even if you don't believe my words! Then you would come to experience me and be convinced that I am in the Father and the Father is in me."

[39]Once again they attempted to seize him, but he escaped miraculously from their clutches. [40]Then Jesus went back to the place where John had baptized him at the crossing of the Jordan. [41]Many came out to where he was and said about him, "Even though John didn't perform any miracles, everything he predicted about this man is true!" [42]And many people became followers of Jesus at the Jordan and believed in him.

Lazarus Raised from the Dead

11 [1-2]In the village of Bethany there was a man named Lazarus, and his sisters, Mary and Martha. Mary was the one who would anoint Jesus' feet with costly perfume and dry his feet with her long hair. One day Lazarus became very sick to the point of death. [3]So his sisters sent a message

to Jesus, "Lord, our brother Lazarus, the one you love, is very sick. Please come!"

[4]When he heard this, he said, "This sickness will not end in death for Lazarus, but will bring glory and praise to God. This will reveal the greatness of the Son of God by what takes place."

[5-6]Now even though Jesus loved Mary, Martha, and Lazarus, he remained where he was for two more days. [7]Finally, on the third day, he said to his disciples, "Come. It's time to go to Bethany."

[8]"But Teacher," they said to him, "do you really want to go back there? It was just a short time ago the people of Judea were going to stone you!"

[9-10]Jesus replied, "Are there not twelve hours of daylight in every day? You can go through a day without the fear of stumbling when you walk in the One who gives light to the world. But you will stumble when the light is not in you, for you'll be walking in the dark."

[11]Then Jesus added, "Lazarus, our friend, has just fallen asleep. It's time that I go and awaken him."

[12]When they heard this, the disciples replied, "Lord, if he has just fallen asleep, then he'll get better." [13]Jesus was speaking about Lazarus' death, but the disciples presumed he was talking about natural sleep.

[14]Then Jesus made it plain to them, "Lazarus is dead. [15]And for your sake, I'm glad I wasn't there, because now you have another opportunity to see who I am so that you will learn to trust in me. Come, let's go and see him."

16So Thomas, nicknamed the Twin, remarked to the other disciples, "Let's go so that we can die with him."

17-18Now when they arrived at Bethany, which was only about two miles from Jerusalem, Jesus found that Lazarus had already been in the tomb for four days. 19Many friends of Mary and Martha had come from the region to console them over the loss of their brother. 20And when Martha heard that Jesus was approaching the village, she went out to meet him, but Mary stayed in the house.

21Martha said to Jesus, "My Lord, if only you had come sooner, my brother wouldn't have died. 22But I know that if you were to ask God for anything, he would do it for you."

23Jesus told her, "Your brother will rise and live."

24She replied, "Yes, I know he will rise with everyone else on resurrection day."

25"Martha," Jesus said, "You don't have to wait until then. I am the Resurrection, and I am Life Eternal. Anyone who clings to me in faith, even though he dies, will live forever. 26And the one who lives by believing in me will never die. Do you believe this?"

27Then Martha replied, "Yes, Lord, I do! I've always believed that you are the Anointed One, the Son of God who has come into the world for us!" 28Then she left and hurried off to her sister, Mary, and called her aside from all the mourners and whispered to her, "The Master is here and he's asking for you."

29So when Mary heard this, she quickly went off to find him, 30for Jesus was lingering outside the village at the same spot where Martha met him. 31Now when Mary's friends who were comforting her noticed how quickly she ran out of the house, they followed her, assuming she was going to the tomb of her brother to mourn.

³²When Mary finally found Jesus outside the village, she fell at his feet in tears and said, "Lord, if only you had been here, my brother would not have died."

³³When Jesus looked at Mary and saw her weeping at his feet, and all her friends who were with her grieving, he shuddered with emotion and was deeply moved with tenderness and compassion. ³⁴He said to them, "Where did you bury him?"

"Lord, come with us and we'll show you," they replied.

³⁵Then tears streamed down Jesus' face.

³⁶Seeing Jesus weep caused many of the mourners to say, "Look how much he loved Lazarus." ³⁷Yet others said, "Isn't this the One who opens blind eyes? Why didn't he do something to keep Lazarus from dying?"

³⁸Then Jesus, with intense emotions, came to the tomb—a cave with a stone placed over its entrance. ³⁹Jesus told them, "Roll away the stone."

Then Martha said, "But Lord, it's been four days since he died—by now his body is already decomposing!"

⁴⁰Jesus looked at her and said, "Didn't I tell you that if you will believe in me, you will see God unveil his power?"

⁴¹So they rolled away the heavy stone. Jesus gazed into heaven and said, "Father, thank you that you have heard my prayer, ⁴²for you listen to every word I speak. Now, so that these who stand here with me will believe that you have sent me to the earth as your messenger, I will use the power you

have given me." ⁴³Then with a loud voice Jesus shouted with authority: "Lazarus! Come out of the tomb!"

⁴⁴Then in front of everyone, Lazarus, who had died four days earlier, slowly hobbled out—he still had grave clothes tightly wrapped around his hands and feet and covering his face! Jesus said to them, "Unwrap him and let him loose."

⁴⁵From that day forward many of those who had come to visit Mary believed in him, for they had seen with their own eyes this amazing miracle! ⁴⁶But a few went back to inform the Pharisees about what Jesus had done.

⁴⁷So the Pharisees and the chief priests called a special meeting of the High Council and said, "So what are we going to do about this man? Look at all the great miracles he's performing! ⁴⁸If we allow him to continue like this, everyone will believe in him. And the Romans will take action and destroy both our country and our people!"

⁴⁹Now Caiaphas, the high priest that year, spoke up and said, "You don't understand a thing! ⁵⁰Don't you realize we'd be much better off if this one man were to die for the people than for the whole nation to perish?"

⁵¹(This prophecy that Jesus was destined to die for the Jewish people didn't come from Caiaphas himself, but he was moved by God to prophesy as the chief priest. ⁵²And Jesus' death would not be for the Jewish people only, but to gather together God's children scattered around the world and unite them as one.) ⁵³So from that day on, they were committed to killing Jesus.

⁵⁴For this reason Jesus no longer went out in public among

the Jews. But he went in the wilderness to a village called Ephraim, where he secluded himself with his disciples.

⁵⁵Now the time came for the Passover preparations, and many from the countryside went to Jerusalem for their ceremonial cleansing before the feast began. ⁵⁶And all the people kept looking out for Jesus, expecting him to come to the city. They said to themselves while they waited in the temple courts, "Do you think that he will dare come to the feast?" ⁵⁷For the leading priests and the Pharisees had given orders that they be informed immediately if anyone saw Jesus, so they could seize and arrest him.

Mary Anoints Jesus

12 Six days before the Passover began, Jesus went back to Bethany, the town where he raised Lazarus from the dead. ²They had prepared a supper for Jesus. Martha served, and Lazarus and Mary were among those at the table. ³Mary picked up an alabaster jar filled with nearly a liter of extremely rare and costly perfume—the purest extract of nard, and she anointed Jesus' feet. Then she wiped them dry with her long hair. And the fragrance of the costly oil filled the house. ⁴But Judas the locksmith, Simon's son, the betrayer, spoke up and said, ⁵"What a waste! We could have sold this perfume for a fortune and given the money to the poor!"

⁶(In fact, Judas had no heart for the poor. He only said this because he was a thief and in charge of the money case. He would steal money whenever he wanted from the funds given to support Jesus' ministry.)

⁷Jesus said to Judas, "Leave her alone! She has saved it for the time of my burial. ⁸You'll always have the poor with you; but you won't always have me."

⁹When the word got out that Jesus was not far from Jerusalem, a large crowd came out to see him, and they also wanted to see Lazarus, the man Jesus had raised from the dead. ¹⁰This prompted the chief priests to seal their plans to do away with both Jesus and Lazarus, ¹¹for his miracle testimony was incontrovertible and was persuading many of the Jews living in Jerusalem to believe in Jesus.

¹²The next day the news that Jesus was on his way to Jerusalem swept through the massive crowd gathered for the feast. ¹³So they took palm branches and went out to meet him. Everyone was shouting, "Lord, be our Savior! Blessed is the one who comes to us sent from Jehovah-God, the King of Israel!"

¹⁴Then Jesus found a young donkey and rode on it to fulfill what was prophesied: ¹⁵"People of Zion, have no fear! Look—it's your king coming to you riding on a young donkey!"

¹⁶Now Jesus' disciples didn't fully understand the importance of what was taking place, but after he was raised and exalted into glory, they understood how Jesus fulfilled all the prophecies in the Scriptures that were written about him.

¹⁷All the eyewitnesses of the miracle Jesus performed when he called Lazarus out of the tomb and raised him from the dead kept spreading the news about Jesus to everyone. ¹⁸The news of this miracle of resurrection caused the crowds to swell as great numbers of people welcomed him into the city with joy. ¹⁹But the Pharisees were disturbed by this and

said to each other, "We won't be able to stop this. The whole world is going to run after him!"

True Seekers

20Now there were a number of foreigners from among the nations who were worshipers at the feast. 21They went to Philip (who came from the village of Bethsaida in Galilee) and they asked him, "Would you take us to see Jesus? We want to see him." 22So Philip went to find Andrew, and then they both went to inform Jesus.

23He replied to them, "Now is the time for the Son of Man to be glorified. 24Let me make this clear: A single grain of wheat will never be more than a single grain of wheat unless it drops into the ground and dies. Because then it sprouts and produces a great harvest of wheat—all because one grain died.

25"The person who loves his life and pampers himself will miss true life! But the one who detaches his life from this world and abandons himself to me, will find true life and enjoy it forever! 26If you want to be my disciple, follow me and you will go where I am going. And if you truly follow me as my disciple, the Father will shower his favor upon your life.

27"Even though I am torn within, and my soul is in turmoil, I will not ask the Father to rescue me from this hour of trial. For I have come to fulfill my purpose—to offer myself to God. 28So, Father, bring glory to your name!" Then suddenly a booming voice was heard from the sky,

> "I have glorified my name! And I will glorify it through you again!"

29The audible voice of God startled the crowd standing nearby. Some thought it was only thunder, yet others said, "An angel just spoke to him!"

30Then Jesus told them, "The voice you heard was not for my benefit, but for yours—to help you believe. 31From this moment on, everything in this world is about to change, for the ruler of this dark world will be overthrown. 32And I will do this when I am lifted up off the ground and when I draw the hearts of people to gather them to me." 33He said this to indicate that he would die by being lifted up on the cross.

34People from the crowd spoke up and said, "Die? How could the Anointed One die? The Word of God says that the Anointed One will live with us forever, but you just said that the Son of Man must be lifted up from the earth. And who is this Son of Man anyway?"

35Jesus replied, "You will have the light shining with you for only a little while longer. While you still have me, walk in the light, so that the darkness doesn't overtake you. For when you walk in the dark you have no idea where you're going. 36So believe and cling to the light while I am with you, so that you will become children of light." After saying this, Jesus then entered into the crowd and hid himself from them.

The Unbelief of the Crowd

37Even with the overwhelming evidence of all the many signs and wonders that Jesus had performed in front of them, his critics still refused to believe. 38This fulfilled the prophecy given by Isaiah:

Lord, who has believed our message? Who has seen the unveiling of your great power?

39And the people were not able to believe, for Isaiah also prophesied:

40God has blinded their eyes and hardened their hearts to the truth. So with their eyes and hearts closed they cannot understand the truth nor turn to me so that I could instantly cleanse and heal them.

41Isaiah said these things because he had seen and experienced the splendor of Jesus and prophesied about him. 42Yet there were many Jewish leaders who believed in Jesus, but because they feared the Pharisees they kept it secret, so they wouldn't be ostracized by the assembly of the Jews. 43For they loved the glory that men could give them rather than the glory that came from God!

Jesus' Last Public Teaching

44Jesus shouted out passionately, "To believe in me is to also believe in God who sent me. 45For when you look at me you are seeing the One who sent me. 46I have come as a light to shine in this dark world so that all who trust in me will no longer wander in darkness. 47If you hear my words and refuse to follow them, I do not judge you. For I have not come to judge you but to save you. 48If you reject me and refuse to follow my words, you already have a judge. The message of truth I have given you will rise up to judge you at the Day of Judgment. 49For I'm not speaking as someone who is self-appointed, but I speak by the authority of the Father himself who sent me, and who instructed me what to say. [50]And I know that the Father's commands result in eternal life, and that's why I speak the very words I've heard him speak."

Jesus Washes Feet

13 Jesus knew that the night before Passover would be his last night on earth before leaving this world to return to the Father's side. All throughout his time with his disciples, Jesus had demonstrated a deep and tender love for them. And now he longed to show them the full measure of his love. [2]Before their evening meal had begun, the accuser had already planted betrayal into the heart of Judas Iscariot, the son of Simon.

[3]Now Jesus was fully aware that the Father had placed all things under his control, for he had come from God and was about to go back to be with him. [4]So he got up from the meal and took off his outer robe, and took a towel and wrapped it around his waist. [5]Then he poured water into a basin and began to wash the disciples' dirty feet and dry them with his towel.

[6]But when Jesus got to Simon Peter, he objected and said, "I can't let you wash my dirty feet—you're my Lord!"

[7]Jesus replied, "You don't understand yet the meaning of what I'm doing, but soon it will be clear to you."

[8]Peter looked at Jesus and said, "You'll never wash my dirty feet—never!"

"But Peter, if you don't allow me to wash your feet," Jesus responded, "then you will not be able to share life with me."

[9]So Peter said, "Lord, in that case, don't just wash my feet, wash my hands and my head too!"

10Jesus said to him, "You are already clean. You've been washed completely and you just need your feet to be cleansed—but that can't be said of all of you." For Jesus knew which one was about to betray him, 11and that's why he told them that not all of them were clean.

12After washing their feet, he put his robe on and returned to his place at the table. "Do you understand what I just did?" Jesus said. 13"You've called me your teacher and lord, and you're right, for that's who I am. 14–15So if I'm your teacher and lord and have just washed your dirty feet, then you should follow the example that I've set for you and wash one another's dirty feet. Now do for each other what I have just done for you. 16I speak to you timeless truth: a servant is not superior to his master, and an apostle is never greater than the one who sent him. 17So now put into practice what I have done for you, and you will experience a life of happiness enriched with untold blessings!"

Jesus Predicts His Betrayal

18"I don't refer to all of you when I tell you these things, for I know the ones I've chosen—to fulfill the Scripture that says, 'The one who shared supper with me treacherously betrays me.' 19I am telling you this now, before it happens, so that when the prophecy comes to pass you will be convinced that I AM. 20"Listen to this timeless truth: whoever receives the messenger I send receives me, and the one who receives me receives the Father who sent me."

21Then Jesus was moved deeply in his spirit. Looking at his

disciples, he announced, "I tell you the truth—one of you is about to betray me."

²²Eyeing each other, his disciples puzzled over which one of them could do such a thing. ²³The disciple that Jesus dearly loved was at the right of him at the table and was leaning his head on Jesus. ²⁴Peter gestured to this disciple to ask Jesus who it was he was referring to. ²⁵Then the dearly loved disciple leaned into Jesus' chest and whispered, "Master, who is it?"

²⁶"The one I give this piece of bread to after I've dipped it in the bowl," Jesus replied. Then he dipped the piece of bread into the bowl and handed it to Judas Iscariot, the son of Simon. ²⁷And when Judas ate the piece of bread, Satan entered him. Then Jesus looked at Judas and said, "What you are planning to do, go do it now." ²⁸None of those around the table realized what was happening. ²⁹Some thought that Judas, their trusted treasurer, was being told to go buy what was needed for the Passover celebration, or perhaps to go give something to the poor. ³⁰So Judas left quickly and went out into the dark night to betray Jesus.

Jesus Predicts Peter's Denial

³¹After Judas left the room, Jesus said, "The time has come for the glory of God to surround the Son of Man, and God will be greatly glorified through what happens to me. ³²And very soon God will unveil the glory of the Son of Man.

³³"My dear friends, I only have a brief time left to be with you. And then you will search and long for me. But I tell you what I told the Jewish leaders: you'll not be able to come where I am.

³⁴"So I give you now a new commandment: Love each other just as much as I have loved you. ³⁵For when you demonstrate the same love I have for you by loving one another, everyone will know that you're my true followers."

³⁶Peter interjected, "But, Master, where are you going?"

Jesus replied, "Where I am going you won't be able to follow, but one day you will follow me there."

³⁷Peter said, "What do you mean I'm not able to follow you now? I would sacrifice my life to die for you!"

³⁸Jesus answered, "Would you really lay down your life for me, Peter? Here's the absolute truth: Before the rooster crows in the morning, you will say three times that you don't even know me!"

Jesus Comforts His Disciples

14 "Don't worry or surrender to your fear. For you've believed in God, now trust and believe in me also. ²My Father's house has many dwelling places. If it were otherwise, I would tell you plainly, because I go to prepare a place for you to rest. ³And when everything is ready, I will come back and take you to myself so that you will be where I am. ⁴And you already know the way to the place where I'm going."

⁵Thomas said to him, "Master, we don't know where you're going, so how could we know the way there?"

⁶Jesus explained, "I am the Way, I am the Truth, and I am the Life. No one comes next to the Father except through union with me. To know me is to know my Father too. ⁷And from now on you will realize that you have seen him and experienced him."

8Philip spoke up, "Lord, show us the Father, and that will be all that we need!"

9Jesus replied, "Philip, I've been with you all this time and you still don't know who I am? How could you ask me to show you the Father, for anyone who has looked at me has seen the Father. 10Don't you believe that the Father is living in me and that I am living in the Father? Even my words are not my own but come from my Father, for he lives in me and performs his miracles of power through me. 11Believe that I live as one with my Father and that my Father lives as one with me—or at least, believe because of the mighty miracles I have done.

12"I tell you this timeless truth: The person who follows me in faith, believing in me, will do the same mighty miracles that I do—even greater miracles than these because I go to be with my Father! 13For I will do whatever you ask me to do when you ask me in my name. And that is how the Son will show what the Father is really like and bring glory to him. 14Ask me anything in my name, and I will do it for you!"

Jesus Prophesies about the Holy Spirit

15"Loving me empowers you to obey my commands. 16-17And I will ask the Father and he will give you another Savior, the Holy Spirit of Truth, who will be to you a friend just like me—and he will never leave you. The world won't receive him because they can't see him or know him. But you will know him intimately, because he will make his home in you and will live inside you.

18"I promise that I will never leave you helpless or abandon you as orphans—I will come back to you! ¹⁹Soon I will leave this world and they will see me no longer, but you will see me, because I will live again, and you will come alive too. ²⁰So when that day comes, you will know that I am living in the Father and that you are one with me, for I will be living in you. ²¹Those who truly love me are those who obey my commands. Whoever passionately loves me will be passionately loved by my Father. And I will passionately love you in return and will manifest my life within you."

²²Then one of the disciples named Judas (not Judas Iscariot) said, "Lord, why is it you will only reveal your identity to us and not to everyone?"

²³Jesus replied, "Loving me empowers you to obey my word. And my Father will love you so deeply that we will come to you and make you our dwelling place. ²⁴But those who don't love me will not obey my words. The Father did not send me to speak my own revelation, but the words of my Father. ²⁵I am telling you this while I am still with you. ²⁶But when the Father sends the Spirit of Holiness, the One like me who sets you free, he will teach you all things in my name. And he will inspire you to remember every word that I've told you.

²⁷"I leave the gift of peace with you—my peace. Not the kind of fragile peace given by the world, but my perfect peace. Don't yield to fear or be troubled in your hearts—instead, be courageous! ²⁸"Remember what I've told you, that I must go away, but I promise to come back to you. So if you truly love me, you will be glad for me, since I'm returning to my Father, who is greater than I. ²⁹So when all of these things happen, you will still trust and cling to me. ³⁰I won't

speak with you much longer, for the ruler of this dark world is coming. But he has no power over me, for he has nothing to use against me. ³¹I am doing exactly what the Father destined for me to accomplish, so that the world will discover how much I love my Father. Now come with me."

Jesus the Living Vine

15 "I am a true sprouting vine, and the farmer who tends the vine is my Father. ²He cares for the branches connected to me by lifting and propping up the fruitless branches and pruning every fruitful branch to yield a greater harvest. ³The words I have spoken over you have already cleansed you. ⁴So you must remain in life-union with me, for I remain in life-union with you. For as a branch severed from the vine will not bear fruit, so your life will be fruitless unless you live your life intimately joined to mine.

⁵"I am the sprouting vine and you're my branches. As you live in union with me as your source, fruitfulness will stream from within you—but when you live separated from me you are powerless. ⁶If a person is separated from me, he is discarded; such branches are gathered up and thrown into the fire to be burned. ⁷But if you live in life-union with me and if my words live powerfully within you—then you can ask whatever you desire and it will be done. ⁸When your lives bear abundant fruit, you demonstrate that you are my mature disciples who glorify my Father!

⁹"I love each of you with the same love that the Father loves me. You must continually let my love nourish your hearts. ¹⁰If you keep my commands, you will live in my love,

just as I have kept my Father's commands, for I continually live nourished and empowered by his love. [11]My purpose for telling you these things is so that the joy that I experience will fill your hearts with overflowing gladness!

[12]"So this is my command: Love each other deeply, as much as I have loved you. [13]For the greatest love of all is a love that sacrifices all. And this great love is demonstrated when a person sacrifices his life for his friends.

[14]"You show that you are my intimate friends when you obey all that I command you. [15]I have never called you 'servants,' because a master doesn't confide in his servants, and servants don't always understand what the master is doing. But I call you my most intimate friends, for I reveal to you everything that I've heard from my Father. [16]You didn't choose me, but I've chosen and commissioned you to go into the world to bear fruit. And your fruit will last, because whatever you ask of my Father, for my sake, he will give it to you! [17]So this is my parting command: Love one another deeply!"

True Disciples Can Expect Persecution

[18]"Just remember, when the unbelieving world hates you, they first hated me. [19]If you were to give your allegiance to the world, they would love and welcome you as one of their own. But because you won't align yourself with the values of this world, they will hate you. I have chosen you and taken you out of the world to be mine. [20]So remember what I taught you, that a servant isn't superior to his master. And since they persecuted me, they will also persecute you. And

if they obey my teachings, they will also obey yours. 21They will treat you this way because you are mine, and they don't know the One who sent me.

22"If I had not come and revealed myself to the unbelieving world, they would not feel the guilt of their sin, but now their sin is left uncovered. 23If anyone hates me, they hate my Father also. 24If I had not performed miracles in their presence like no one else has done, they would not feel the guilt of their sins. But now, they have seen and hated both me and my Father. 25And all of this has happened to fulfill what is written in their Scriptures: They hated me for no reason.

26"And I will send you the Divine Encourager from the very presence of my Father. He will come to you, the Spirit of Truth, emanating from the Father, and he will speak to you about me. 27And you will tell everyone the truth about me, for you have walked with me from the start."

Jesus Warns His Disciples

16 "I have told you this so that you would not surrender to confusion or doubt. 2For you will be excommunicated from the synagogues, and a time is coming when you will be put to death by misguided ones who will presume to be doing God a great service by putting you to death. 3And they will do these things because they don't know anything about the Father or me. 4I'm telling you this now so that when their time comes you will remember that I foretold it. I didn't tell you this in the beginning because I was still with you. 5But now that I'm about to leave you and go back to join the One who sent me, you need to be told. Yet, not one of

you are asking me where I'm going. ⁶Instead your hearts are filled with sadness because I've told you these things. ⁷But here's the truth: It's to your advantage that I go away, for if I don't go away the Divine Encourager will not be released to you. But after I depart, I will send him to you. ⁸And when he comes, he will expose sin and prove that the world is wrong about God's righteousness and his judgments.

⁹"'Sin,' because they refuse to believe in who I am.

¹⁰"God's 'righteousness,' because I'm going back to join the Father and you'll see me no longer.

¹¹"And 'judgment' because the ruler of this dark world has already received his sentence.

¹²"There is so much more I would like to say to you, but it's more than you can grasp at this moment. ¹³But when the truth-giving Spirit comes, he will unveil the reality of every truth within you. He won't speak his own message, but only what he hears from the Father, and he will reveal prophetically to you what is to come. ¹⁴He will glorify me on the earth, for he will receive from me what is mine and reveal it to you. ¹⁵Everything that belongs to the Father belongs to me—that's why I say that the Divine Encourager will receive what is mine and reveal it to you. ¹⁶Soon you won't see me any longer, but then, after a little while, you will see me in a new way."

¹⁷Some of the disciples asked each other, "What does he mean, 'Soon you won't see me,' and, 'A little while after that and you will see me in a new way'? And what does he mean, 'Because I'm going to my Father'?" ¹⁸So they kept on repeating, "What's the meaning of 'a little while'? We have no clue what he's talking about!"

¹⁹Jesus knew what they were thinking, and it was obvious that they were anxious to ask him what he had meant, so he spoke up and said, ²⁰"Let me make it quite clear: You will weep and be overcome with grief over what happens to me. The unbelieving world will be happy, while you will be filled with sorrow. But know this, your sadness will turn into joy when you see me again! ²¹Just like a woman giving birth experiences intense labor pains in delivering her baby, yet after the child is born she quickly forgets what she went through because of the overwhelming joy of knowing that a new baby has been born into the world.

²²"So will you also pass through a time of intense sorrow when I am taken from you, but you will see me again! And then your hearts will burst with joy, with no one being able to take it from you! ²³For here is eternal truth: When that time comes you won't need to ask me for anything, but instead you will go directly to the Father and ask him for anything you desire and he will give it to you, because of your relationship with me. ²⁴Until now you've not been bold enough to ask the Father for a single thing in my name, but now you can ask, and keep on asking him! And you can be sure that you'll receive what you ask for, and your joy will have no limits!

²⁵"I have spoken to you using figurative language, but the time is coming when I will no longer teach you with veiled speech, but I will teach you about the Father with your eyes unveiled. ²⁶And I will not need to ask the Father on your behalf, for you'll ask him directly because of your new relationship with me. ²⁷For the Father tenderly loves you, because you love me and believe that I've come from God. ²⁸I came

to you sent from the Father's presence, and I entered into the created world, and now I will leave this world and return to the Father's side."

²⁹His disciples said, "At last you're speaking to us clearly and not using veiled speech and metaphors! ³⁰Now we understand that you know everything there is to know, and we don't need to question you further. And everything you've taught us convinces us that you have come directly from God!"

³¹Jesus replied, "Now you finally believe in me. ³²And the time has come when you will all be scattered, and each one of you will go your own way, leaving me alone! Yet I am never alone, for the Father is always with me. ³³And everything I've taught you is so that the peace which is in me will be in you and will give you great confidence as you rest in me. For in this unbelieving world you will experience trouble and sorrows, but you must be courageous, for I have conquered the world!"

Jesus Finished the Father's Work

17 This is what Jesus prayed as he looked up into heaven, "Father, the time has come.
Unveil the glorious splendor of your Son
so that I will magnify your glory!
²You have already given me authority
over all people so that I may give
the gift of eternal life to all those that you have given
to me.
³Eternal life means to know and experience you
as the only true God,

and to know and experience Jesus Christ,
as the Son whom you have sent.
⁴I have glorified you on the earth
by faithfully doing everything you've told me to do.
⁵So my Father, restore me back to the glory
that we shared together when we were face-to-face
before the universe was created."

Jesus Prays for His Disciples

⁶"Father, I have manifested who you really are
and I have revealed you to the men and women
that you gave to me.
They were yours, and you gave them to me,
and they have fastened your Word firmly to their hearts.
⁷And now at last they know that everything I have is a gift
from you,
⁸And the very words you gave to me to speak
I have passed on to them.
They have received your words
and carry them in their hearts.
They are convinced that I have come from your presence,
and they have fully believed that you sent me to represent you.
⁹So with deep love, I pray for my disciples.
I'm not asking on behalf of the unbelieving world,
but for those who belong to you,
those you have given me.
¹⁰For all who belong to me now belong to you.

And all who belong to you now belong to me as well,
and my glory is revealed through their surrendered
lives.

[11]"Holy Father, I am about to leave this world
to return and be with you,
but my disciples will remain here.
So I ask that by the power of your name,
protect each one that you have given me,
and watch over them so that they will be united
as one, even as we are one.

[12]While I was with these that you have given me,
I have kept them safe by your name that you have given
me.
Not one of them is lost,
except the one that was destined to be lost,
so that the Scripture would be fulfilled.

[13]"But now I am returning to you so Father,
I pray that they will experience
and enter into my joyous delight in you
so that it is fulfilled in them and overflows.

[14]I have given them your message
and that is why the unbelieving world hates them.
For their allegiance is no longer to this world
because I am not of this world.

[15]I am not asking that you remove them from the world,
but I ask that you guard their hearts from evil,

[16]For they no longer belong to this world any more than
I do.

[17]"Your Word is truth! So make them holy by the truth.

¹⁸I have commissioned them to represent me
    just as you commissioned me to represent you.
¹⁹And now I dedicate myself to them as a holy sacrifice
    so that they will live as fully dedicated to God
    and be made holy by your truth."

Jesus Prays for You

²⁰"And I ask not only for these disciples,
    but also for all those who will one day
    believe in me through their message.
²¹I pray for them all to be joined together as one
    even as you and I, Father, are joined together as one.
    I pray for them to become one with us
    so that the world will recognize that you sent me.
²²For the very glory you have given to me I have given them
    so that they will be joined together as one
    and experience the same unity that we enjoy.
²³You live fully in me and now I live fully in them
    so that they will experience perfect unity,
    and the world will be convinced that you have sent me,
    for they will see that you love each one of them
    with the same passionate love that you have for me.
²⁴"Father, I ask that you allow everyone that you have given
    to me
    to be with me where I am!
    Then they will see my full glory—
    the very splendor you have placed upon me
    because you have loved me even before the beginning
    of time.

²⁵"You are my righteous Father,
   but the unbelieving world has never known you
   in the perfect way that I know you!
   And all those who believe in me
   also know that you have sent me!
²⁶I have revealed to them who you are
   and I will continue to make you even more real to them,
   so that they may experience the same endless love
   that you have for me,
   for your love will now live in them, even as I live in
      them!"

Jesus in the Garden of Gethsemane

18 After Jesus finished this prayer; he left with his disciples and went across the Kidron Valley to a place where there was a garden. ²Judas, the traitor, knew where this place was, for Jesus had gone there often with his disciples. ³The Pharisees and the leading priests had given Judas a large detachment of Roman soldiers and temple police to seize Jesus. Judas guided them to the garden, all of them carrying torches and lanterns and armed with swords and spears. ⁴Jesus, knowing full well what was about to happen, went out to the garden entrance to meet them. Stepping forward, he asked, "Who are you looking for?"

⁵"Jesus of Nazareth," they replied. (Now Judas, the traitor, was among them.)

He replied, "I am he."

⁶And the moment Jesus spoke the words, "I am he," the mob fell backward to the ground!

7So once more, Jesus asked them, "Who are you looking for?"

As they stood up, they answered, "Jesus of Nazareth."

8Jesus replied, "I told you that I am the one you're looking for, so if you want me, let these men go home."

9He said this to fulfill the prophecy he had spoken, "Father, not one of those you have given me has been lost."

10Suddenly, Peter took out his sword and struck the high priest's servant, slashing off his right ear! The servant's name was Malchus.

11Jesus ordered Peter, "Put your sword away! Do you really think I will avoid the suffering which my Father has assigned to me?"

Jesus Is Taken before Annas

12Then the soldiers and their captain, along with the Jewish officers, seized Jesus and tied him up. 13They took him first to Annas, as he was the father-in-law of Caiaphas, the high priest that year. 14Caiaphas was the one who had persuaded the Jewish leaders that it would be better off to have one person die for the sake of the people.

Peter's First Denial

15Peter and another disciple followed along behind them as they took Jesus into the courtyard of Annas' palace. Since the other disciple was well known to the high priest, he entered in, 16but Peter was left standing outside by the gate. Then the other disciple came back out to the servant girl who was guarding the gate and convinced her to allow Peter inside. [17]As he passed inside, the young servant girl guarding the gate took a look at Peter and said to him, "Aren't you one of his disciples?"

He denied it, saying, "No! I'm not!"

[18]Now because it was cold, the soldiers and guards made a charcoal fire and were standing around it to keep warm. So Peter huddled there with them around the fire.

Jesus Interrogated by Annas

[19]The high priest interrogated Jesus concerning his disciples and his teachings.

[20]Jesus answered Annas' questions by saying, "I have said nothing in secret. At all times I have taught openly and publicly in a synagogue, in the temple courts, and wherever the people assemble. [21]Why would you ask me for evidence to condemn me? Ask those who have heard what I've taught. They can tell you."

[22]Just then one of the guards standing near Jesus punched him in the face with his fist and said, "How dare you answer the high priest like that!"

[23]Jesus replied, "If my words are evil, then prove it. But if I haven't broken any laws, then why would you hit me?"

[24]Then Annas sent Jesus, still tied up, across the way to the high priest Caiaphas.

Peter's Second and Third Denials

[25]Meanwhile, Peter was still standing in the courtyard by the fire. And one of the guards standing there said to him, "Aren't you one of his disciples? I know you are!" Peter swore and

said, "I am not his disciple!" [26]But one of the servants of the high priest, a relative to the man whose ear Peter had cut off, looked at him and said, "Wait! Didn't I see you out there in the garden with Jesus?" [27]Then Peter denied it the third time and said, "No!"—and at that very same moment, a rooster crowed nearby.

Pilate Questions Jesus' Arrest

[28]Before dawn they took Jesus from his trial before Caiaphas to the Roman governor's palace. Now the Jews refused to go into the Roman governor's residence to avoid ceremonial defilement before eating the Passover meal. [29]So Pilate came outside where they waited and asked them pointedly, "Tell me, what exactly is the accusation that you bring against this man? What has he done?"

[30]They answered, "We wouldn't be coming here to hand over this 'criminal' to you if he wasn't guilty of some wrong-doing!"

[31]Pilate said, "Very well, then you take him yourselves and go pass judgment on him according to your Jewish laws!"

But the Jewish leaders complained and said, "We don't have legal authority to put anyone to death. You should have him crucified!" [32](This was to fulfill the words of Jesus when he predicted the manner of death that he would die.)

Pilate Interrogates Jesus

[33]Upon hearing this, Pilate went back inside his palace and summoned Jesus. Looking him over, Pilate asked him, "Are you really the king of the Jews?"

³⁴Jesus replied, "Are you asking because you really want to know, or are you only asking this because others have said it about me?"

³⁵Pilate responded, "Only a Jew would care about this; do I look like a Jew? It's your own people and your religious leaders that have handed you over to me. So tell me, Jesus, what have you done wrong?"

³⁶Jesus looked at Pilate and said, "The royal power of my kingdom realm doesn't come from this world. If it did, then my followers would be fighting to the end to defend me from the Jewish leaders. My kingdom realm authority is not from this realm."

³⁷Then Pilate responded, "Oh, so then you are a king?"

"You are right." Jesus said, "I was born a King, and I have come into this world to prove what truth really is. And everyone who loves the truth will receive my words."

³⁸Pilate looked at Jesus and said, "What is truth?"

As silence filled the room, Pilate went back out to where the Jewish leaders were waiting and said to them, "He's not guilty. I couldn't even find one fault with him. ³⁹Now, you do know that we have a custom that I release one prisoner every year at Passover—shall I release your king—the king of the Jews?"

⁴⁰They shouted out over and over,' "No, not him! Give us Barabbas!" (Now Barabbas was a robber and a troublemaker.)

Jesus Is Flogged

19 Then Pilate ordered Jesus to be brutally beaten with a whip of leather straps embedded with metal. ²And the soldiers also wove thorn-branches into a crown and set

it on his head and placed a purple robe over his shoulders. ³Then, one by one, they came in front of him to mock him by saying, "Hail, to the king of the Jews!" And one after the other, they repeatedly punched him in the face.

⁴Once more Pilate went out and said to the Jewish officials, "I will bring him out once more so that you know that I've found nothing wrong with him." ⁵So when Jesus emerged, bleeding, wearing the purple robe and the crown of thorns on his head, Pilate said to them, "Look at him! Here is your man!"

⁶No sooner did the high priests and the temple guards see Jesus that they all shouted in a frenzy, "Crucify him! Crucify him!"

Pilate replied, "You take him then and nail him to a cross yourselves! I told you—he's not guilty! I find no reason to condemn him."

⁷The Jewish leaders shouted back, "But we have the Law! And according to our Law, he must die, because he claimed to be the Son of God!"

⁸Then Pilate was greatly alarmed when he heard that Jesus claimed to be the Son of God! ⁹So he took Jesus back inside and said to him, "Where have you come from?" But once again, silence filled the room. ¹⁰Perplexed, Pilate said, "Are you going to play deaf? Don't you know that I have the power to grant you your freedom or nail you to a tree?"

¹¹Jesus answered, "You would have no power over me at all, unless it was given to you from above. This is why the one who betrayed me is guilty of an even greater sin."

¹²From then on Pilate tried to find a way out of the situa-

tion and to set him free, but the Jewish authorities shouted him down: "If you let this man go, you're no friend of Caesar! Anyone who declares himself a king is an enemy of the emperor!"

[13]So when Pilate heard this threat, he relented and had Jesus, who was torn and bleeding, brought outside. Then he went up the elevated stone platform and took his seat on the judgment bench—which in Aramaic is called Gabbatha, or "The Bench." [14]And it was now almost noon. And it was the same day they were preparing to slay the Passover lambs.

Then Pilate said to the Jewish officials, "Look! Here is your king!"

[15]But they screamed out, "Take him away! Take him away and crucify him!"

Pilate replied, "Shall I nail your king to a cross?"

The high priests answered, "We have no other king but Caesar!"

[16]Then Pilate handed Jesus over to them. So the soldiers seized him and took him away to be crucified.

Jesus Is Crucified

[17]Jesus carried his own cross out of the city to the place called "The Skull," which in Aramaic is Golgotha. [18]And there they nailed him to the cross. He was crucified, along with two others, one on each side with Jesus in the middle. [19-20]Pilate had them post a sign over the cross, which was written in three languages—Aramaic, Latin, and Greek. Many of the people of Jerusalem read the sign, for he was crucified near the city. The sign stated: "Jesus of Nazareth, the King of the Jews."

21But the chief priests of the Jews said to Pilate, "You must change the sign! Don't let it say, 'King of the Jews,' but rather—'he claimed to be the King of the Jews!'" 22Pilate responded, "What I have written will remain!"

23Now when the soldiers crucified Jesus, they divided up his clothes into four shares, one for each of them. But his tunic was seamless, woven from the top to the bottom as a single garment. 24So the soldiers said to each other, "Don't tear it—let's throw dice to see who gets it!" The soldiers did all of this not knowing they fulfilled the Scripture that says, "They divided my garments among them and gambled for my garment."

25Mary, Jesus' mother, was standing next to his cross, along with Mary's sister, Mary the wife of Clopas, and Mary Magdalene. 26So when Jesus looked down and saw the disciple he loved standing with her, he said, "Mother, look—John will be a son to you." 27Then he said, "John, look—she will be a mother to you!" From that day on, John accepted Mary into his home as one of his own family.

Jesus' Death on the Cross

28Jesus knew that his mission was accomplished, and to fulfill the Scripture, Jesus said: "I am thirsty."

29A jar of sour wine was sitting nearby, so they soaked a sponge with it and put it on the stalk of hyssop and raised it to his lips. 30When he had sipped the sour wine, he said, "It is finished, my bride!" Then he bowed his head and surrendered his spirit to God.

31The Jewish leaders did not want the bodies of the victims to remain on the cross through the next day, since it was the day of preparation for a very important Sabbath. So they asked Pilate's permission to have the victims' legs broken to hasten their death and their bodies taken down before sunset. 32So the soldiers broke the legs of the two men who were nailed there. 33But when they came to Jesus, they realized that he had already died, so they decided not to break his legs. 34But one of the soldiers took a spear and pierced Jesus' side, and blood and water gushed out.

35(I, John, do testify to the certainty of what took place, and I write the truth so that you might also believe.) 36For all these things happened to fulfill the prophecies of the Scriptures:

"Not one of his bones will be broken,"

37and, "They will gaze on the one they have pierced!"

Jesus' Burial

38After this, Joseph from the city of Ramah, who was a secret disciple of Jesus for fear of the Jewish authorities, asked Pilate if he could remove the body of Jesus. So Pilate granted him permission to remove the body from the cross. 39Now Nicodemus, who had once come to Jesus privately at night, accompanied Joseph, and together they carried a significant amount of myrrh and aloes to the cross. 40Then they took Jesus' body and wrapped it in strips of linen with the embalming spices according to the Jewish burial customs. 41Near the place where Jesus was crucified was a garden, and in the garden there was a new tomb where no one had yet been laid to rest. 42And because the Sabbath was approaching, and the tomb was nearby, that's where they laid the body of Jesus.

The Empty Tomb

20 Very early Sunday morning, before sunrise, Mary Magdalene made her way to the tomb. And when she arrived she discovered that the stone that sealed the entrance to the tomb was moved away! ²So she went running as fast as she could to go tell Peter and the other disciple, the one Jesus loved. She told them, "They've taken the Lord's body from the tomb, and we don't know where he is!"

³Then Peter and the other disciple jumped up and ran to the tomb to go see for themselves. ⁴They started out together, but the other disciple outran Peter and reached the tomb first. ⁵He didn't enter the tomb, but peeked in, and saw only the linen cloths lying there. ⁶Then Peter came behind him and went right into the tomb. He too noticed the linen cloths lying there, ⁷but the burial cloth that had been on Jesus' head had been rolled up and placed separate from the other cloths.

⁸Then the other disciple who had reached the tomb first went in, and after one look, he believed! ⁹For until then they hadn't understood the Scriptures that prophesied that he was destined to rise from the dead. ¹⁰Puzzled, Peter and the other disciple then left and went back to their homes.

¹¹Mary arrived back at the tomb, broken and sobbing. She stooped to peer inside, and through her tears ¹²she saw two angels in dazzling white robes, sitting where Jesus' body had been laid—one at the head and one at the feet!

¹³"Dear woman, why are you crying?" they asked.

Mary answered, "They have taken away my Lord, and I don't know where they've laid him."

¹⁴Then she turned around to leave, and there was Jesus standing in front of her, but she didn't realize that it was him!

¹⁵He said to her, "Dear woman, why are you crying? Who are you looking for?"

Mary answered, thinking he was only the gardener, "Sir, if you have taken his body somewhere else, tell me, and I will go and . . ."

¹⁶"Mary," Jesus interrupted her.

Turning to face him, she said, "Rabboni!" (Aramaic for "my teacher")

¹⁷Jesus cautioned her, "Mary, don't hold on to me now, for I haven't yet ascended to God, my Father. And he's not only my Father and God, but now he's your Father and your God! Now go to my brothers and tell them what I've told you, that I am ascending to my Father—and your Father, to my God—and your God!"

¹⁸Then Mary Magdalene left to inform the disciples of her encounter with Jesus. "I have seen the Lord!" she told them. And she gave them his message.

Jesus Appears to His Disciples

¹⁹That evening, the disciples gathered together. And because they were afraid of reprisals from the Jewish leaders, they had locked the doors to the place where they met. But suddenly Jesus appeared among them and said, "Peace to you!" ²⁰Then he showed them the wounds of his hands and his

side—they were overjoyed to see the Lord with their own eyes!

21 Jesus repeated his greeting, "Peace to you!" And he told them, "Just as the Father has sent me, I'm now sending you." 22Then, taking a deep breath, he blew on them and said, "Receive the Holy Spirit. 23I send you to preach the forgiveness of sins—and people's sins will be forgiven. But if you don't proclaim the forgiveness of their sins, they will remain guilty."

Jesus Appears to Thomas

24One of the twelve wasn't present when Jesus appeared to them—it was Thomas, whose nickname was "the Twin." 25So the disciples informed him, "We have seen the Lord with our own eyes!"

Still unconvinced, Thomas replied, "There's no way I'm going to believe this unless I personally see the wounds of the nails in his hands, touch them with my finger, and put my hand into the wound of his side where he was pierced!"

26Then eight days later, Thomas and all the others were in the house together. And even though all the doors were locked, Jesus suddenly stood before them! "Peace to you," he said.

27Then, looking into Thomas' eyes, he said, "Put your finger here in the wounds of my hands. Here—put your hand into my wounded side and see for yourself. Thomas, don't give in to your doubts any longer, just believe!"

28Then the words spilled out of his heart—"You are my Lord, and you are my God!"

²⁹Jesus responded, "Thomas, now that you've seen me, you believe. But there are those who have never seen me with their eyes but have believed in me with their hearts, and they will be blessed even more!"

³⁰Jesus went on to do many more miraculous signs in the presence of his disciples, which are not even included in this book. ³¹But all that is recorded here is so that you will fully believe that Jesus is the Anointed One, the Son of God, and that through your faith in him you will experience eternal life by the power of his name!

Jesus Appears at Lake Galilee

21 Later, Jesus appeared once again to a group of his disciples by Lake Galilee. ²It happened one day while Peter, Thomas (the Twin), Nathanael (from Cana in Galilee), Jacob, John, and two other disciples were all together. ³Peter told them, "I'm going fishing." And they all replied, "We'll go with you." So they went out and fished through the night, but caught nothing.

⁴Then at dawn, Jesus was standing there on the shore, but the disciples didn't realize that it was him! ⁵He called out to them, saying, "Hey guys! Did you catch any fish?"

"Not a thing," they replied.

⁶Jesus shouted to them, "Throw your net over the starboard side, and you'll catch some!" And so they did as he said, and they caught so many fish they couldn't even pull in the net!

⁷Then the disciple whom Jesus loved said to Peter, "It's the Lord!" When Peter heard him say that, he quickly wrapped his outer garment around him, and because he was athletic,

he dove right into the lake to go to Jesus! 8The other disciples then brought the boat to shore, dragging their catch of fish. They weren't far from land, only about a hundred meters. 9And when they got to shore, they noticed a charcoal fire with some roasted fish and bread. 10Then Jesus said, "Bring some of the fish you just caught."

11So Peter waded into the water and helped pull the net to shore. It was full of many large fish, exactly one hundred and fifty-three, but even with so many fish, the net was not torn.

12"Come, let's have some breakfast," Jesus said to them.

And not one of the disciples needed to ask who it was, because every one of them knew it was the Lord. 13Then Jesus came close to them and served them the bread and the fish. 14This was the third time Jesus appeared to his disciples after his resurrection.

Jesus Restores Peter

15After they had breakfast, Jesus said to Peter, "Simon, son of John, do you burn with love for me more than these?"

Peter answered, "Yes, Lord! You know that I have great affection for you!"

"Then take care of my lambs," Jesus said.

16Jesus repeated his question the second time, "Simon, son of John, do you burn with love for me?"

Peter answered, "Yes, my Lord! You know that I have great affection for you!"

"Then take care of my sheep," Jesus said.

¹⁷Then Jesus asked him again, "Peter, son of John, do you have great affection for me?"

Peter was saddened by being asked the third time and said, "My Lord, you know everything. You know that I burn with love for you!"

Jesus replied, "Then feed my lambs! ¹⁸Peter, listen, when you were younger you made your own choices and you went where you pleased. But one day when you are old, others will tie you up and escort you where you would not choose to go—and you will spread out your arms." ¹⁹(Jesus said this to Peter as a prophecy of what kind of death he would die, for the glory of God.) And then he said, "Peter, follow me!"

²⁰Then Peter turned and saw that the disciple whom Jesus loved was following them. (This was the disciple who sat close to Jesus at the Last Supper and had asked him, "Lord, who is the one that will betray you?") ²¹So when Peter saw him, he asked Jesus, "What's going to happen to him?"

²²Jesus replied, "If I decide to let him live until I return, what concern is that of yours? You must still keep on following me!"

²³So the rumor started to circulate among the believers that this disciple wasn't going to die. But Jesus never said that, he only said, "If I let him live until I return, what concern is that of yours?"

Conclusion

²⁴I, John, am that disciple who has written these things to testify of the truth, and we know that what I've documented is

accurate. [25] Jesus did countless things that I haven't included here. And if every one of his works were written down and described one by one, I suppose that the world itself wouldn't have enough room to contain the books that would have to be written!

About
The Passion Translation

The message of God's story is timeless; the Word of God doesn't change. But the methods by which that story is communicated should be timely; the vessels that steward God's Word can and should change.

One of those timely methods and vessels is Bible translation. Bible translations are both a gift and a problem. They give us the words God spoke through his servants, but words can be very poor containers for revelation because they leak! The meanings of words change from one generation to the next. Meaning is influenced by culture, background, and many other details. You can imagine how differently the authors of the Bible saw the world two thousand years ago.

There is no such thing as a truly literal translation of the Bible, for there is not an equivalent language that perfectly conveys the meaning of the biblical text except as it is understood in its original cultural and linguistic setting. Therefore, a translation can be a problem. The problem, however, is solved when we seek to transfer meaning, not merely words, from the original text to the receptor language.

The Passion Translation seeks to reintroduce the passion and fire of the Bible to the English reader by expressing God's passion for people and his world, translating the original, life-changing message of God's Word for modern readers.

ITALICIZED WORDS AND HEBREW NAMES

You will notice at times we've italicized certain words or phrases. These highlighted portions are not in the original Hebrew, Greek, or Aramaic manuscripts, but are implied from the context. We've made these implications explicit for the sake of narrative clarity and to better convey the meaning of God's Word. This is a common practice by mainstream translations, including the New American Standard Bible and King James Version.

We've also chosen to translate certain names in their original Hebrew or Greek form to better convey their cultural meaning and significance. For instance, translations of the Bible have substituted Jacob with James. Both Greek and Aramaic leave the Hebrew names in their original form. Therefore this translation uses Jacob throughout.

———

God longs to have his Word expressed in every language in a way that would unlock the passion of his heart. Our goal is to trigger inside every English speaker an overwhelming response to the truth of the Bible. This is a heart-level translation, from the passion of God's heart to the passion of your heart.

We pray and trust that this version of God's Word will kindle in you a burning, passionate desire for him and his heart, while impacting the world for years to come!

God's Promises from the Book of John

Assurance

"But everyone my Father has given to me, they will come. And all who come to me, I will embrace and will never turn them away." (6:37)

"'My own sheep will hear my voice and I know each one, and they will follow me. I give to them the gift of eternal life and they will never be lost and no one has the power to snatch them out of my hands. My Father, who has given them to me as his gift, is the mightiest of all, and no one has the power to snatch them from my Father's care. The Father and I are one." (10:27–30)

"Eternal life means to know and experience you as the only true God, and to know and experience Jesus Christ, as the Son whom you have sent." (17:3)

Belief

Jesus shouted out passionately, "To believe in me is to also believe in God who sent me. For when you look at me you are seeing the One who sent me. I have come as a light to shine in this dark world so that all who trust in me will no longer wander in darkness." (12:44–46)

Then, looking into Thomas' eyes, he said, "Put your finger here in the wounds of my hands. Here—put your hand into my wounded side and see for yourself. Thomas, don't give in to your doubts any longer, just believe!" Then the words spilled out of his heart—"You are my Lord, and you are my God! Jesus responded, "Thomas, now that you've seen me, you believe. But there are those who have never seen me with their eyes but have believed in me with their hearts, and they will be blessed even more!" (20:27–29)

Jesus went on to do many more miraculous signs in the presence of his disciples, which are not even included in this book. But all that is recorded here is so that you will fully believe that Jesus is the Anointed One, the Son of God, and that through your faith in him you will experience eternal life by the power of his name! (20:30–31)

Blessing

"If you want to be my disciple, follow me and you will go where I am going. And if you truly follow me as my disciple, the Father will shower his favor upon your life." (12:26)

"I speak to you timeless truth: a servant is not superior to his master, and an apostle is never greater than the one who sent him. So now put into practice what I have done for you, and you will experience a life of happiness enriched with untold blessings!" (13:16–17)

Calling

"I tell you this timeless truth: The person who follows me in faith, believing in me, will do the same mighty miracles that I do—even greater miracles than these because I go to be with my Father!" (14:12)

"You didn't choose me, but I've chosen and commissioned you to go into the world to bear fruit. And your fruit will last, because whatever you ask of my Father, for my sake, he will give it to you!" (15:16)

Jesus repeated his greeting, "Peace to you!" And he told them, "Just as the Father has sent me, I'm now sending you." (20:21)

Condemnation

"So now there is no longer any condemnation for those who believe in him, but the unbeliever already lives under condemnation because they do not believe in the name of God's beloved Son." (3:18)

"I speak to you an eternal truth: if you embrace my message and believe in the One who sent me, you will never face condemnation, for in me, you have already passed from the realm of death into the realm of eternal life!" (5:24)

Until finally, Jesus was left alone with the woman still standing there in front of him. So he stood back up and said to her, "Dear woman, where are your accusers? Is there no one here to condemn you?"

Looking around, she replied, "I see no one, Lord."

Jesus said, "Then I certainly don't condemn you either. Go, and from now on, be free from a life of sin." (8:10–11)

Comfort

"Don't worry or surrender to your fear. For you've believed in God, now trust and believe in me also." (14:1)

"And everything I've taught you is so that the peace which is in me will be in you and will give you great confidence as you rest in me. For in this unbelieving world you will experience trouble and sorrows, but you must be courageous, for I have conquered the world!" (16:33)

Death

"I speak to you eternal truth: Soon the dead will hear the voice of the Son of God, and those who listen will arise with life!" (5:25)

"I speak to you this eternal truth: whoever cherishes my words and keeps them will never experience death." (8:51)

Deliverance

"I speak eternal truth," Jesus said. "When you sin you are not free. You've become a slave in bondage to your sin. And slaves have no permanent standing in a family, like a son does, for a son is a part of the family forever. So if the Son sets you free from sin, then become a true son and be unquestionably free!" (8:34–36)

Eternal Life

"For this is how much God loved the world—he gave his one and only, unique Son as a gift. So now everyone who believes in him will never perish but experience everlasting life." (3:16)

"I speak to you an eternal truth: if you embrace my message and believe in the One who sent me, you will never face condemnation, for in me, you have already passed from the realm of death into the realm of eternal life!" (5:24)

"For the longing of my Father is that everyone who embraces the Son and believes in him will experience eternal life and I will raise them up in the last day!" (6:40)

Forgiveness

The very next day John saw Jesus coming to him to be baptized, and John cried out, "Look! There he is—God's Lamb! He will take away the sins of the world!" (1:29)

"I send you to preach the forgiveness of sins—and people's sins will be forgiven. But if you don't proclaim the forgiveness of their sins, they will remain guilty." (20:23)

Freedom

Jesus said to those Jews who believed in him, "When you continue to embrace all that I teach, you prove that you are my true followers. For if you embrace the truth, it will release more freedom into your lives." (8:31–32)

Guidance

Then Jesus said, "I am light to the world and those who embrace me will experience life-giving light, and they will never walk in darkness." (8:12)

"There is so much more I would like to say to you, but it's more than you can grasp at this moment. But when the truth-giving Spirit comes, he will unveil the reality of every truth within you. He won't speak his own message, but only what he hears from the Father, and he will reveal prophetically to you what is to come." (16:12–13)

Heaven

"My Father's house has many dwelling places. If it were otherwise, I would tell you plainly, because I go to prepare a place for you to rest. And when everything is ready, I will come back and take you to myself so that you will be where I am." (14:2–3)

Help

Jesus answered, "I speak an eternal truth: Unless you are born of water and Spirit-wind, you will never enter God's kingdom realm. For the natural realm can only give birth to things that are natural, but the spiritual realm gives birth to supernatural life! (3:5–6)

"Loving me empowers you to obey my commands. And I will ask the Father and he will give you another Savior, the Holy Spirit of Truth, who will be to you a friend just like me—and he will never leave you. The world won't receive him because they can't see him or know him. But you will know him intimately, because he will make his home in you and will live inside you." (14:15–17)

"But here's the truth: It's to your advantage that I go away, for if I don't go away the Divine Encourager will not be released to you. But after I depart, I will send him to you. And when he comes, he will expose sin and prove that the world is wrong about God's righteousness and his judgments." (16:7–8)

Joy

"My purpose for telling you these things is so that the joy that I experience will fill your hearts with overflowing gladness!" (15:11)

"So will you also pass through a time of intense sorrow when I am taken from you, but you will see me again! And then your hearts will burst with joy, with no one being able to take it from you!" (16:22)

Life

Jesus said to them, "I am the Bread of Life. Come every day to me and you will never be hungry. Believe in me and you will never be thirsty." (6:35)

"A thief has only one thing in mind—he wants to steal, slaughter, and destroy. But I have come to give you everything in abundance, more than you expect—life in its fullness until you overflow!" (10:10)

Love

"So I give you now a new commandment: Love each other just as much as I have loved you. For when you demonstrate the same love I have for you by loving one another, everyone will know that you're my true followers."(13:34–35)

"Those who truly love me are those who obey my commands. Whoever passionately loves me will be passionately loved by my Father. And I will passionately love you in return and will manifest my life within you." (14:21)

""I love each of you with the same love that the Father loves me. You must continually let my love nourish your hearts. If you keep my commands, you will live in my love, just as I have kept my Father's commands, for I continually live nourished and empowered by his love." (15:9–10)

"You live fully in me and now I live fully in them
so that they will experience perfect unity,
and the world will be convinced that you have sent me,
for they will see that you love each one of them
with the same passionate love that you have for me."
    (17:23)

Obedience

So Jesus responded, "I don't teach my own ideas, but the truth revealed to me by the One who sent me. If you want to test my teachings and discover where I received them, first be passionate to do God's will, and then you will be able to discern if my teachings are from the heart of God or from my own opinions." (7:16–17)

"If you hear my words and refuse to follow them, I do not judge you. For I have not come to judge you but to save you. If you reject me and refuse to follow my words, you already have a judge. The message of truth I have given you will rise up to judge you at the Day of Judgment. For I'm not speaking as someone who is self-appointed, but I speak by

the authority of the Father himself who sent me, and who instructed me what to say." (12:47–49)

"You show that you are my intimate friends when you obey all that I command you." (15:14)

Peace

"I leave the gift of peace with you—my peace. Not the kind of fragile peace given by the world, but my perfect peace. Don't yield to fear or be troubled in your hearts—instead, be courageous!" (14:27)

Power

"I am the sprouting vine and you're my branches. As you live in union with me as your source, fruitfulness will stream from within you—but when you live separated from me you are powerless." (15:5)

Prayer

"For I will do whatever you ask me to do when you ask me in my name. And that is how the Son will show what the Father is really like and bring glory to him. 14Ask me anything in my name, and I will do it for you!" (14:13–14)

"But if you live in life-union with me and if my words live powerfully within you—then you can ask whatever you desire and it will be done." (15:7)

"You didn't choose me, but I've chosen and commissioned you to go into the world to bear fruit. And your fruit will last, because whatever you ask of my Father, for my sake, he will give it to you!" (15:16)

"For here is eternal truth: When that time comes you won't need to ask me for anything, but instead you will go directly to the Father and ask him for anything you desire and he will give it to you, because of your relationship with me. 24Until now you've not been bold enough to ask the Father for a single thing in my name, but now you can ask, and keep on asking him! And you can be sure that you'll receive what you ask for, and your joy will have no limits!" (16:23–24)

Relationship

"My own sheep will hear my voice and I know each one, and they will follow me." (10:27)

Jesus explained, "I am the Way, I am the Truth, and I am the Life. No one comes next to the Father except through union with me. To know me is to know my Father too." (14:6)

"I have never called you 'servants,' because a master doesn't confide in his servants, and servants don't always understand what the master is doing. But I call you my most intimate friends, for I reveal to you everything that I've heard from my Father." (15:15)

Resurrection

"For just like the Father has power to raise the dead, the Son will raise the dead and give life to whomever he wants." (5:21)

"And I have come out of heaven not for my own desires, but for the satisfaction of my Father who sent me. My Father who sent me has determined that I will not lose even one of those he has given to me, and I will raise them up in the last day." (6:38–39)

"I am the Resurrection, and I am Life Eternal. Anyone who clings to me in faith, even though he dies, will live forever. 26And the one who lives by believing in me will never die. Do you believe this?" (11:25–26)

Rescue

But those who embraced him and took hold of his name were given authority to become the children of God! (1:12)

"God did not send his Son into the world to judge and condemn the world, but to be its Savior and rescue it!" (3:17)

"I am the Gateway. To enter through me is to experience life, freedom, and satisfaction." (10:9)

Satisfaction

Jesus answered, "If you drink from Jacob's well you'll be thirsty again and again, but if anyone drinks the living water I give them, they will never thirst again and will be forever satisfied! For when you drink the water I give you it becomes a gushing fountain of the Holy Spirit, springing up and flooding you with endless life!" (4:13–14)

Jesus said to them, "I am the Bread of Life. Come every day to me and you will never be hungry. Believe in me and you will never be thirsty." (6:35)

Then on the most important day of the feast, the last day, Jesus stood and shouted out to the crowds—"All you thirsty ones, come to me! Come to me and drink! [38]Believe in me so that rivers of living water will burst out from within you, flowing from your innermost being, just like the Scripture says!" (7:37–38)

Truth

Jesus said to those Jews who believed in him, "When you continue to embrace all that I teach, you prove that you are my true followers. For if you embrace the truth, it will release more freedom into your lives." (8:31–32)

Jesus explained, "I am the Way, I am the Truth, and I am the Life. No one comes next to the Father except through union with me. To know me is to know my Father too." (14:6)

"But when the truth-giving Spirit comes, he will unveil the reality of every truth within you. He won't speak his own message, but only what he hears from the Father, and he will reveal prophetically to you what is to come. He will glorify me on the earth, for he will receive from me what is mine and reveal it to you. Everything that belongs to the Father belongs to me—that's why I say that the Divine Encourager will receive what is mine and reveal it to you." (16:13–15)

Worship

"From here on, worshiping the Father will not be a matter of the right place but with the right heart. For God is a Spirit, and he longs to have sincere worshipers who worship and adore him in the realm of the Spirit and in truth." (4:23–24)

Your Story with Jesus

How God longs for us to know him! We discover him as we read and study his living Word. But the "Word" is not just dead letters; it's the Living Expression of God, Jesus Christ. The Word came with skin on as the Perfect Man—the One who is the divine self-expression and fullness of God's glory; he was God in the flesh!

There are three things that are important to remember about John, the author of this gospel: First, he was a man who was a passionate follower of Jesus Christ. He had seen the miracles of Jesus firsthand and heard the anointed words he taught. He walked with Jesus and followed him wholeheartedly, becoming one of Christ's apostolic servants.

Secondly, John described himself as "the disciple whom Jesus loved." This was not a term to indicate that Jesus loved John more than the others, but rather, John saw himself as one that Jesus loved. You could also say this about yourself, "I am the disciple whom Jesus loves!" Every believer can echo John's description of himself, as those words must become the true definition of our identity.

Love unlocks mysteries. As we love Jesus, our hearts are unlocked to see more of his beauty and glory. When we stop defining ourselves by our failures, but rather as the one whom Jesus loves, then our hearts begin to open to the breathtaking discovery of the wonder of Jesus Christ.

And thirdly, it's important to keep in mind that John did not include everything that Jesus did and taught. In fact, if you put all the data of the Gospels together and condense it, we only have information covering merely a few months of Jesus' life and ministry! We are only given snapshots, portions of what he taught, and a few of the miracles he performed. From his birth to the age of twelve, we know virtually nothing about his life; and from the age of twelve until he began his public ministry at thirty, we again have almost no information given to us about him in the Gospels. John summarizes his incomplete account in the last verse of his gospel:

Jesus did an untold number of other things than what I've included here. And if every one of his deeds were written down and described one by one, I suppose that the world itself wouldn't have enough room for the books that would have to be written. (21:25)

According to one of the church fathers, Tertullian, John was plunged in burning oil in front of a massive crowd that had filled the Roman Coliseum in order to silence his ministry. But God was not yet finished with his aged apostle.

Tertullian reports that he came out of the burning cauldron alive and unharmed! This miracle resulted in the mass conversion to Christ of nearly all who witnessed it. John was later banished to the island of Patmos where he wrote the book of the Revelation of Jesus Christ.

The gospel of John is all about the beautiful Christ. John told us why he wrote this amazing book:

But all that is recorded here is so that you will fully believe that Jesus is the Anointed One, the Son of God, and that through your faith in him you will experience eternal life by the power of his name! (20:31)

The purpose of this book is to help people to believe that Jesus is the One through whom they will find and experience eternal life and the fullness of that life by Jesus' powerful name. The word *believe* is found one hundred times in John. It is the gospel of believing! The Bible proclaims that Jesus Christ is the Living Expression of God and the Light of the World. He is the Savior, the King, the true Anointed One, the Living Bread, and the Loving Shepherd.

Will you believe today?

You can invite Jesus into your life—for the first time or to renew your commitment—by saying a prayer like this:

Jesus, I want to follow you. My sins have separated me from you. I believe that you love me. Thank you for paying the price for my sins, and I trust your finished work on the cross for my rescue. Forgive me and awaken my heart to love you with all my heart, mind, soul, and strength. I believe God raised you from the dead, and I want that new life to fill me each day and for eternity. God, I give you my life. Fill me with your Spirit so that my life honors you and I fulfill your purpose for my life. Amen.

WHAT'S NEXT?

You can be assured that what Jesus said about people who choose to follow him is true: "If you embrace my message and believe in the One who sent me, you will never face condemnation, for in me, you have already passed from the realm of death into the realm of eternal life!" (5:24)

But there's more! Not only are you declared "Not guilty!" by God because of Jesus, you are also considered his most intimate friend (15:15).

To help you in your new life, God provides you his Spirit, "who will be to you a friend...and he will never leave you" (14:16-17). And Jesus says, "I leave you the gift of peace with you—my peace. Not the kind of fragile peace given by the world, but my perfect peace" (14:27).

Here are three things you can do next to grow in your relationship with Jesus:

- *Stay Connected to God.* Jesus said, "I am the sprouting vine and you're my branches. As you live in union with me as your source, fruitfulness will stream from within you—but when you live separated from me you are powerless" (15:5). The two best ways to remain connected to Jesus is by regularly reading the Bible and communicating with God through prayer. (Visit thePassionTranslation.com to learn more about other books of the Bible available in this translation.)

- *Seek Obedience.* Jesus also invites you to obey his teachings, which is how we show we love him: "Those who truly love me are those who obey my commandments" (14:21). When we do obey him, Jesus promises we will remain in God's love, a love that empowers us to obey him: "If you keep my commands, you will live in my love, just as I have kept my Father's commands, for I continually live nourished and empowered by his love." The Holy Spirit will make your spirit aware of what is right and wrong. Listen and follow what he shows you.

- *Find Community.* Finally, Jesus tells us it's important to unite with his other followers for encouragement, companionship, and growth: "I pray for them all to be joined together as one even as you and I, Father, are joined together as one" (17:21). And in this fellowship, Jesus says we are to "love each other just as much as I have loved you" (13:34). Find a church or a gathering of believers in Jesus who obey God's Word and follow Jesus passionately.

Continue to talk to Jesus each day, follow him, and discover that his eternal love is always available for you. Your life will never be the same after absorbing the glory presented to you in the book of John.

Notes

Notes

Notes

Notes

Notes

Notes

Notes

thePassionTranslation.com